£2.50

HUNTING

AND

FISHING

HONORÉ DAUMIER

HUNTING

AND

FISHING

PREFACE
PAUL VIALAR

CATALOGUE AND NOTES
JACQUELINE ARMINGEAT

LEON AMIEL PUBLISHER, INC.

PARIS - NEW YORK

TRANSLATED FROM THE FRENCH BY HOWARD BRABYN

ISBN 08 148 0642 2

© ÉDITIONS ANDRÉ SAURET, 1975

PRINTED IN FRANCE

Not even the most unobservant or most uncritical of men can live in a world or a society such as ours without becoming aware of its oddities or being amused or irritated by the behaviour of those of whom it is composed.

Amused or repelled by the life that surrounds them, or impelled by their natural disposition, there are those who, taking up the writer's pen or artist's crayon, produce a candid, often caustic, portrait of the eccentricities or misdeeds of the protagonists of this never-ending comedy—at times it turns to drama—which they colour with mocking laughter or expressions of disgust.

Honoré Daumier was one of these; and if we trace the artist-caricaturist's life, we find that it follows a steady course. For a short period after the Revolution of 1848, a strangely uncharacteristic change of heart drew him back for a time to the paths of artistic conformity, some would say to the paths of wisdom, from which, it must be admitted, he very soon strayed once more.

He was twenty-four years old and a contributor to *La Caricature* when, in 1832, his biting *Gargantua,* a caricature of a king feasting gluttonously on taxpayers' money (a monarch who bore a close resemblance to the reigning sovereign of France, Louis-Philippe) earned him a six-month spell in prison. Ministers, deputies, permanent office-holders, all felt the cruel lash of his skilled hand, and beneath their portraits, which at times he signed with the pseudonym Rogelin, could be found such vilifications as: "Members of the Chamber of Prostitutes". But perhaps Daumier's victims had become accustomed to the violence of his attacks. He suffered no further imprisonment and, giving himself free rein, he spared no one. There was no escape from his remorseless pursuit for *Les assassins de la rue de Vaugirard* (The assassins of the Rue de Vaugirard), the *Divorceuses* (The match-breakers), the *Philanthropes* (The philanthropists), the *Bons bourgeois* (The middle-class), the *Propriétaires* (Men of property), the *Actionnaires* (Shareholders) whom he depicted at *La Pêche* (Fishing), nor was he less severe with the *Bals de cour* (Court balls), or the *Pastorales.*

As mentioned earlier, for a period after 1848, Daumier turned solemn, even conventional, with his pictures of *La République qui nourrit ses enfants et les instruit* (The Republic that nurtures and instructs its children). It could not last; society offered him too many targets for satire and his paintings of contemporary life throw a pitiless and uncompromising light on a whole era, its trades and functions, as well on individuals from every walk of life.

He did not, however, stop there. From classic antiquity, whose absurdities he stressed, to his "actualités" (news items), a kind of intimate, personal journal in which he recounted the salient news and points of interest of each day, up to those pictures of contemporary life, drawn in vitriol perhaps but still a faithful representation of his age, he has bequeathed us a burlesque, uncompromising panorama of a period which, without him, we would know only from the reports of his over-complacent contemporaries who preferred to shut their eyes and pretend to themselves that they lived in the best of worlds.

The anglers and hunting folk found in this anthology form part of Daumier's panorama of the life of his day.

It is probably true that he was less well acquainted with them than with the people from the worlds of the theatre, medicine or politics, whose fads, defects, vices, fatuity and pomposity aroused his often-justified venom. Here the biting mockery gives way to a gentler, at times almost indulgent, smile. His artist's crayon, no longer vengeful, becomes almost friendly. What a pity he never encountered those strange characters one meets at businessmen's shooting parties, those pseudo-sportsmen, invited guns, whose money enables them to buy shares in a business or in a grouse moor.

First let us take a look at fishing, which certainly has its place in this book. The anglers Daumier shows us lining the banks of the Seine bear comparison with the line of marksmen at a shoot. Over the heads of these " sportsmen", for whom pulling a trigger is synonymous with hunting, beaters despatch ducks specially raised to be slaughtered, pheasants fattened up in hen runs to become "game birds" and often bought the day before from the man who reared them, scarcely able to fly as they emerge from their coops to be prodded forward with kicks and blows towards the line of guns.

Had he known of these practices, had he seen these "sportsmen" whose targets are more poultry than game, how Daumier's harsh crayon would have anathematized this caricature of what should be a noble sport and these men who belie their manhood for the sake of an ephemeral pleasure.

The same sometimes holds true, alas, with angling. Yet one can scarcely beat trout towards the man with rod and line in his hand, short of letting him fish in a fish-pond. Besides, there is the whole art of angling, the choice of the right spot in the right river, the selection of the right fly which varies with every hour of the day, the art of casting.

How splendid it would have been if Daumier had had an insight into all this. He could have used his knowledge to administer a few corrections, as he did to other people in other fields.

I can see him now, with pencil poised, sketching the two characters in the following well-known anecdote.

Two men, both stone deaf, both encumbered from head to foot with innumerable rods, lines, baskets, in fact all the accoutrements of the compleat angler, meet on the bank of a river. The first man says to the other:

—"Ah! You are going fishing!"

The other man, who has not heard a word, replies:

—"No. I am going fishing."

To which the first man, who hasn't heard a word either, answers:

—"I thought you were going fishing."

It seems to me that the same deaf misunderstanding exists among those who can envisage and practice the sports of fishing or shooting only with the aid of all those facilities that the pseudo-sportsman all too readily makes use of. This is perhaps less true of those who fish for sport, some, indeed many, of whom practice the art in the right spirit. It is, however, only too true of the man who, once he has a gun in his hand, thinks that he can do as he pleases and joins in the kind of shooting party I have described above.

It is above all the uncomplaining resignation and the more comical aspect of the angler that emerges from Daumier's sketches. Both aspects are heavily underlined in his sketch of a fisherman in shirt-sleeves who has been waiting for two hours for a bite without noticing that in making his cast he has caught his line in the willow above him and who remarks that since he has been there the fish have stopped biting.

Uncomplaining resignation is also the chief quality of the angler up to his waist in water, a kingfisher of the Seine like his counterpart *The Old Angler,* who stays in the icy waves, his rod in front of him, and who, in the words of Daumier's caption, *like the independent-minded, persevering, uncomplaining man he is, is not discouraged by adversity and*

8

battles against all the difficulties that encompass him, suffering storm and tempest in philosophical silence.

Daumier also must have seen the persistent angler who, though he has been without success for hours, still hopes for the miracle of the big catch he will never achieve.

We have all seen wives, like those depicted by Daumier, who, whether through devotion or because they are obliged to, go with their husbands and wait for hours on end so that they can bear witness to the story to be recounted later of that rare miracle, which occurs only on special days, of the landing of an exceptional pike, carp or trout which will grow in size as the years go by. Stoical and uncomplaining in their own way under the rain, they ask timidly: "Don't you think we ought to go?" only to hear in reply: "Hortense, I think they are going to start biting... just give me half an hour more". Inevitably the half an hour becomes an hour or even half a day. As Daumier said, a woman must follow her husband wherever he elects to establish his domicile.

Thanks to him we get a view of what angling was like in those days, an ingenuous caricature of sporting exploits that were never achieved, and of the banks of the Seine dotted with anglers every metre, their rods aligned as though on parade. These were men from all walks of life, but even there rank insisted on its prerogatives, as witness the angling club vice-president telling one of his members not to catch a fish before he does himself.

Things have indeed changed. Angling, unlike shooting, has evolved as a sport. Nevertheless, the *aficionados* of the sport who neglect their wives to practice their hobby still run the risk of seeing their wives (it happened in Daumier's day too), alone and abandoned, seek consolation in the arms of an attractive boyfriend.

But it was above all shooting that aroused, and with good reason, the caricaturist's more lively interest.

It must be admitted that although shooting was not the caricaturist's gold mine that it is today, from which he could have extracted more than a few sparkling nuggets, he was certainly aware of the gloriously stupid aspects of those self-styled Nimrods and of their ignorance of nature and the beasts that form part of it—that is, when they were not the domestically-raised variety of which I spoke earlier.

Naive, ignorant and pretentious, shooting merely to be able to say that they went shooting rather than for love of the sport, harassed, anxious, surprised and boastful, finding themselves suddenly placed in dangerous situations, mistaking a sparrow for a pheasant, a dog for a wolf, wondering whether the rabbit they were pursuing and had eluded them had perhaps climbed a tree, picking up the farmyard cock they thought to be a grouse, a sparrow they had confused with a partridge, killing their dog instead of the hare at which they had aimed, or just killing time if they failed to kill anything else, these were the men who composed the caricaturist's portrait gallery, and still do so today.

For in this consumer society in which money is often too quickly acquired, those who are in a position to "go hunting", as they put it, are now legion. These are the people who form the burlesque parade that would have, I am sure, unleashed Honoré Daumier's bitter scorn. For in his day hunting was still, I believe, similar to what it was in my youth—a natural occupation in which one pursued game which had to be flushed out and tracked with only the assistance of a dog.

Yes, indeed, at that time hunting was quite another matter.
"The man who has never experienced long runs astride a horse behind a pack in full cry, through the heart of the forest or skirting ploughed fields, or who has never merely stood at the edge of a wood, early on an autumn morning, a gun resting in the crook of his arm, listening to the cries of the hounds in pursuit of a hare, that man", said old Aristide, shaking his head, "that man, does not know what life is."

This was just his simple way of saying that for him, as for so many others, everything began and ended—and indeed such was his fate—with hunting. I can see him now, his face burnt with the suns of many seasons, his jacket faded by rain and shower, the old huntsman who was to die on the field of battle, killed by a branch in the face at full gallop in pursuit of a "ten-pointer", his skull split like a dry nut, his brain spilling out so pink that it seemed impossible that it could be that of an old man.

Is that life? This sport that some find so terrible? Yes indeed, "for life is only life if there is death", a phrase that is more than a mere platitude.

I have said and written this many times before, but I think that when one talks about hunting, even in connexion with Daumier, it is as well to repeat it for those who have never heard it before and also for those who have forgotten it.

Hunting with a pack, shooting, all forms of the sport are only truly hunting when those who indulge in it respect the unwritten "code of honour" that all real hunters respect. One could modify the famous saying and change it to read "Tell me how you hunt and I shall tell you what sort of a person you are". There is currently some talk of making people pass a test before they can obtain a hunting permit. The idea is a good one, but not only should it be concerned, as is proposed, with matters of safety (breech of the rifle open when not being fired, barrel pointed towards the ground or the sky and not pointed towards the other marksmen), it should also, primarily, be concerned with the morality of hunting: respect for animals and for humanitarian rules which imply that one does not shoot and merely wound or maim an animal and leave it to suffer for days and days in the woods or valleys in which it has taken refuge.

These rules should also forbid the shooting of sitting targets. How Daumier's crayon would have flayed the two members of the Chamber of Deputies in the following anecdote. Invited to a presidential shoot, although they had never held a gun in their hands nor seen a pheasant before, and allocated a place at the edge of a wood, the two men spotted a pheasant walking slowly towards the line of marksmen.

"Look... a pheasant... there in front of you!" cried one. "Well, go on... shoot!"

To which the other man replied:

"No... not yet... I am waiting for it to stand still."

Though doubtless a good and tender father, easily moved to tears, the man was quite unaware that, at that moment, he was about to commit a murder. And if one was to reproach him with this, he would doubtless reply:

"Well, what of it; isn't that what hunting is?"

No, thank goodness, it is something quite different. As Pohu, a tenant-farmer of my childhood days and deputy mayor of the commune which issued me my first hunting licence, used to say to me:

"As your aunt's tenant, my boy" (I often used to accompany him to the woods or fields before I was of an age to carry a gun), "I tell you that holding a gun in your hand is a serious matter. You must have a good reason to take a life, whether of an animal or any other being, and if you do so you must do it while respecting certain rules. Don't confuse the hunter with the meat-merchant and the murderer. If I see a man shoot a sitting bird or hare, I never invite him on to my land again. There are some men of that kind, neighbours of mine though they may be, to whom I will never speak again."

Yes, hunting is quite another matter.

Hunting is seeking out a clever, subtle quarry that has a chance of escape. It is shooting only at an animal in full possession of its faculties and strength and not at a puny rabbit or a baby bird that has not yet learnt to fly. If it were not so, one would only have to go to the nearest hen-coop with a gun and kill and kill again just for the sake of killing. And when, a few years ago, I spoke on television about hunting and said that I did not go hunting to kill, a charming but idiotic young lady journalist who writes for an evening newspaper asked next day in her column: why, then, does he go hunting?

We go hunting for all the other reasons.

We go for the reasons explained by La Verdure, the old huntsman of my youth—to hear the hounds approaching through the woods and wait to see a hare break cover, to watch him zigzagging so skilfully that the guns cannot touch him. We go to walk for hours in search of partridge and then suddenly to hear a covey that had allowed man and dog to pass take flight behind us. We go to greet the snipe that rises from the marsh ahead of us and then takes cover in the sweet-scented reeds from which we will not be able to flush him. We go to try to creep up on the wild goat and the chamois, those daemons of the mountains, or the capercailzie who, like the woodcock in spring, only forgets to watch out for danger or the presence of men during the mating season. To go hunting is to discover life.

It is, above all, to discover nature, vibrant with the life of all creatures and who, like a book that one spells out word by word, gradually reveals the secrets of her fields, her marshes and her forests, a setting which, save for the base of heart, could never be the scene of premeditated murder.

More often than not in this matter there is a confusion between sensitivity and sentimentality. Hunting is a noble sport. The cattle that are taken from the fields to be slaughtered, the chicken that the farmer's wife entices towards her with a few grains of corn and then has its neck severed with a jagged knife kept in the barn, these are purpose-reared as food and are not the conquests of man. We eat these animals to live and this men have always done. "Eat one another" is a commandment which, in the name of a higher morality, men have vainly tried to transform into "Love one another". What comparison is there between the slaughter of a beast that one sees and feeds daily and the rifle shot that, after long and often fruitless tracking, ends the life of a deer as it crosses a forest path, or of a bird that swoops like a flash of lightning from one tree-top to another? That is hunting and that is why we love it. As I have written elsewhere:

"As with any other action, one can only hunt with a pure heart. It is then, and only then, that its beauty and nobility becomes fully apparent. It is only then that it is transformed from an act of death to an act of life. Yes, that is what hunting is, the sport that has given us so much, which we love with all our strength and with all our heart and without which we should be the poorer and a little less men.

I don't know whether Daumier was a hunter. At any rate, he is not guilty of any sentimentality in the drawings he has left us. He lived at a time when hunting and shooting were still commonplace but in which pseudo-sportsmen were already taking up these pastimes with a lack of finesse matched only by their lack of understanding. Nevertheless, one senses in him a certain fondness for those poor unfortunates who traipsed the woods and ploughlands to return, more often than not, emptyhanded. And when the poulterer suggests to one of them who has bagged nothing that as well as a pheasant he might like to buy a "fine lobster" too, this evokes not mocking laughter but a smile as the ingenuousness of the victim outweighs the show of ridicule.

But, as I have said before, how greatly I regret that Daumier the moralist—for moralist he was above all—could not have met some of the preposterous characters of hunting today. What sketches, what vengeful caricatures he would have given us, to judge by the marvellous ones he produced of those characters he did encounter. How splendidly he would have portrayed their accoutrements and their idiosyncrasies.

It has been my lot to meet many of these characters during fifty years of hunting and especially over the last thirty years, that is to say since the end of the last war. Conditions have changed in hunting, not only in our own country but also in Africa where "safaris" are organized by agencies and "hunting brokers" who might just as well be dealers in soup. A voyage to Black Africa costs a lot of money, and, now that money is king, the "market", as one organizer I know bluntly described it, has been flooded with a host of ingenuous, irresponsible, cocksure men with the unshakable confidence in their own ideas that only riches can provide, suddenly promoted to the role, I almost wrote rank, of Nimrod and beside whom Tartarin of Tarascon would have paled into insignificance.

For some, to go hunting gives them status, raises them in the social scale. To buy a share in a grouse moor—they are offered by the score every year in the specialist magazines—of some landowner, preferably titled, who, without their money would be unable to meet the enormous expense involved in the upkeep of his property, the grain for his game, the traps, the fencing, etc., is considered as proof of a rise in their social status. But they come to hunting without being informed, and for very good reasons, of its artificial aspects. In their innocence they believe that this is how it has always been. And how can we reproach them for this when they have known nothing other than what they are offered in exchange for their clinking moneybags? They need to be humble enough to want to learn how they should behave, what they should wear, and to realise that it is not enough to go clay-pigeon shooting in the suburbs of Paris a few times beforehand for them to be able to join the ranks of those who need to ask no questions because they "know".

There is a virtually unending parade of these unwittingly comic, burlesque characters:

The building promoter, that king of concrete and the low-rent apartment block, and his girl friend whom he has bought her first gun although she doesn't know one end of it from the other.

The ex-government minister whose political career is over and who reminisces nostalgically about the presidential hunts to which he used to be invited but to which he will never go again now that the political wind has changed.

The garage owner who arrives with a flourish in a noisy sports car that he hopes to sell later to some simpleton among his fellow invitees.

The banker whose advice is said to be worth its weight in gold—to his clients, but especially to himself—and who receives innumerable invitations for himself and his gloriously stupid, ham-fisted wife in return for his invaluable, sure-fire tips.

The fashionable veterinary surgeon who patches up sick racehorses and who is hoping to tempt some rich gentleman into buying one of them. After all, hunting isn't everything and there are racehorse owners or potential owners for whom "owning a string" is also a sign of social advancement. They too would have gladdened Daumier's heart.

The sub-prefect who, finding himself posted, at the whim of chance and of the government, to a hunting region, sets out to learn to shoot and, thinking he has succeeded, starts shooting in all directions and sighting the partridge as they fly at head level, forcing his neighbours to dive for cover to avoid being blinded by his pellets.

The surgeon, who comes on Sunday to breathe the fresh country air so as to ensure that his hand will hold the scalpel steady on Monday, shooting at the birds as they emerge, myopic, easy targets from their coops, as though getting his hand in on unprotesting patients.

The lawyer, making flourishes with his arms when he shoots, just as though he were in court making dramatic play with the sleeves of his gown, and flexing his knees like a dismounted cavalryman as he waits for the birds to arrive.

The famous shot, an old and impoverished aristocrat, who is only there because no one invites him anywhere else now that he has lost his standing, looking around him with an air of sad condescension.

The district notary, who considers an invitation from a client almost as his due and whose only thought is for the hamper of game that will be handed to him in the evening when the shoot is over and the bag has been counted. His wife awaits the brace of pheasant and the hare that will be distributed to each gun as though it were manna from heaven; she will weigh them thoughtfully in her hand and, as usual, will complain that the hare is too small.

The advertising magnate, who reigns in splendour in a suite at the top of his office block in a famous Avenue in Paris. He sweeps the Avenue with the imperial eye of the man responsible for distributing publicity flashes announcing special offers for "Vericlene" washing-powder or "Dawn Freshness" shaving cream. Yet, as he freely admits, when he first arrived in Paris he used to sweep that same Avenue with a broom.

The following story about him, which I have no hesitation in recounting since it is so typical, is etched forever on my memory. I must add that it took place a long time ago and that, since then, he has learnt a lot.

There are still one or two great, really genuine game preserves where, although some game birds are reared by gamekeepers, this is only done to supplement nature and is necessary to ensure the survival of the breed of pheasant and partridge. Shooting on these preserves is a reasonable, natural form of sport. A single stretch of land is not shot over a score of times and then left permanently denuded of game. Each piece of land is shot over only once and the birds that survive this annual shoot are allowed to live in peace. On the day in question I had been invited to the opening of the partridge season, an occasion which, for many years, had been restricted to a small group of privileged initiates who knew each other well and were all real marksmen and real sports-men. As usual there were eight guns besides our host and we were awaiting the arrival of the tenth gun to complete our party.

He was late, but it was customary not to defer the start of the shoot for late arrivals on the rare occasions when anyone was delayed, since the beaters had to set out at a fixed time from the far end of the plain. It was only when we noticed that one gun was missing that we learnt the name of the absentee. It was the advertising magnate I mentioned earlier.

When he told us his name our host made it clear that the man was new to the sport and that this was to be his first shoot. He had·pressed hard for an invitation and our host had found it difficult to refuse him, especially since one of the guests invited earlier had had to drop out.

We were about to sit down to the quick, light luncheon usually served before the beginning of the shoot, when our host was called to the telephone. On his return he told us:

"That was X" (giving the name of the advertising magnate). "He says that something has gone wrong with his Rolls but that he will soon be here. He is going to come in his Buick."

Half way through luncheon the telephone rang again. It was X to inform us that his wife had borrowed the Buick and that he would be coming in her Alfa Romeo.

He hadn't arrived when we left the table and set out for the shoot. The beaters had made their first sally and we were getting ready for the second, when along the road in the distance we saw a cloud of dust. Soon the vehicle that had raised it pulled up near us just as we were preparing to return to our allotted places in the line. A smart chauffeur in a uniform gleaming with gold buttons leapt out of the car and walked round it, cap in hand, to open the rear door. The belated guest emerged from the low-slung Jaguar in which he had arrived and, with an air of genuine concern, explained that he had really been dogged by bad luck, that his wife had left the Alfa Romeo at their country place and that he had had to send his chauffeur to fetch the Jaguar from the workshop in which it was being serviced.

He was introduced to us all and shook each of us vigorously by the hand. Much moved by the tribulations he had suffered, we examined him more closely.

He was wearing the most beautiful shooting outfit it has been my privilege to see throughout my long sporting career, and one that only a high society tailor could have dreamed up. It had pockets everywhere—in fact we could see nothing but pockets—positioned in the most bizarre and impractical places, pockets which could serve no imaginable purpose. His jacket was made of a sickly-pink material and lined with dove-grey silk. His trousers were a curious cross between bloomers and riding-breeches. His boots were of cream-coloured suede.

"What are we shooting?" he asked, while his chauffeur opened the trunk of the car and drew out an incredible box of paraphernalia.

"Partridge", replied the controller of the shoot.

"O.K., I'll just get my things ready" said the newly-arrived guest as he took the card proffered by our host on which was marked the number of his position in the line.

The rest of us took up our positions. After preparing himself with the utmost care, and taking his time about it, our man walked past us to take up his station at the far end of the line. Like all the others,

I watched fascinated as he passed. Round his waist was slung a magnificent leather bandolier festooned with other leather gadgets which effectively prevented all access to the pockets of his jacket. His servant followed carrying a strange collection of objects and bowed down under the weight of hundreds of cartridges. In addition he was carrying a folding chair, or rather, an upholstered armchair. This was to be literally a matter of "armchair shooting"—which was unlikely to improve the accuracy of his aim. I was astonished to note that he was carrying a Remington five-shot repeater. As he passed he must have read the look of astonishment on my face, for he explained with a sly look:

"This is just the thing for partridge. Five shots without having to reload" (since then this kind of weapon has, luckily, been banned). "Do you realize that means nearly half a pound of lead in the air practically at one time!"

I then asked him if he had often shot partridge. To this he replied that he had not, but that he had spent two or three mornings at a clay-pigeon stand at Meudon to get his hand in. He added:

"The fellow in charge of the stand kept offering me all sorts of advice, but it was a waste of time as I have my own views on the matter."

He certainly had, but they didn't bring him much success that day. He blazed away furiously... but that was all. But he is an intelligent man and has since come to understand things and has learnt a lot. Nowadays he is to be seen at shoots clad in a sober outfit and carrying a good double-barrelled shotgun. And after all, Voltaire also provoked everyone to laughter the first time he went shooting garbed and equipped in grotesque fashion.

And then there is hunting on horseback which is altogether a different affair. Hunting rig is a uniform and it is difficult, except for the occasional tyro—most of them have the good sense to find out the ropes beforehand—to turn up in outlandish attire.

Here tradition is king and not only for those who hunt. Paradoxical as it may seem, this form of hunting is the most democratic of all.

Indeed, anyone who wants to can follow a hunt, even on horseback and not as a member of the hunt. All he has to do is to turn up to the meet, make himself known to the master of the hunt and then follow the hounds, making sure only that he never gets ahead of the master. Peasants, shopkeepers and workmen also often follow the hunt, on bicycles or in small cars. Often they are very knowledgeable about the proceedings. Once a stag has been raised, they often know the precise point at which he will break cover or where he will cross the river. On many occasions these worthy friends from the villages, who could teach a thing or two to many a newly-rich upstart, have asked me:

"Are you coming to *our* hunt next Saturday?"

I was once actually present on a most extraordinary occasion. On that particular day, a powerful stag had been raised and it looked like being an excellent day's hunting and there was a large turn out of enthusiastic followers, on foot, on bicycles and in cars. Unfortunately the run was a short one. By mischance the stag got trapped in a fenced enclosure near a gamekeeper's lodge from which there was no escape. Very soon the crowd gathered round the enclosure and we quickly realized the possible danger to these onlookers should the stag jump the railings and force a way through their packed ranks. A hunt servant came up to the master of the hunt and said:

"Sir, you see the risk we are running. There is liable to be an accident, perhaps even some deaths among the crowd. The game-keeper says we ought to shoot the animal to prevent this."

Now hunting tradition forbids the shooting of an animal in such circumstances. It is the duty of the master of the hunt to give the coup de grâce with his knife and in no other fashion.

"No," replied the master of the hunt, "I forbid it."

At that moment a shot rang out. Fearful of the danger, the game-keeper had levelled his carbine and despatched the animal.

There was an immediate stampede towards the man who had fired the shot. A group of men present threw themselves upon him, beating him and almost lynching him in their anger. There were cries of:

"And what about the tradition?... Have you no respect for the tradition?"

I asked my friend the master of the hunt who these men were, to which he replied:

"Why, they are workmen from the local factory, and most of them are members of the Party too."

Yes, hunting has its rules and traditions and those who know them, whether working-men or men of any other social rank, insist that they must be respected. You will find nothing of the comic or the burlesque among these connoisseurs, these devotees of the sport. For that you will have to look to the newcomers who wear hunting pink thanks only to their money. There are plenty of them and they would have provided a feast for Daumier. Picture one of them—a brand new horn he is unable to sound flapping at his side, over-elegant boots and a piqué cravat spilling out from a canary-yellow waistcoat, bouncing in the saddle and buffeted on his horse like a small boat in a raging sea, moving through the depths of the forest, shaken, red-faced, swollen-veined, clinging desperately to the neck of his mount, understanding nothing of what is going on, unable to distinguish the calls of the horn or a "view halloo" from a "gone away", arriving at the death more dead than the stag. Finally he returns home dog-tired, with a back that will ache for a fortnight, but happy that he will be able to say casually to his big-business or trading acquaintances:

"I was at Lambrefault last week, at the Count's place. He has the finest pack of hounds in France, you know. After a ten-hour run we took a magnificent hart."

There is nothing at all comical, however, about safaris and big-game hunting in Africa. I have already made passing mention and given a brief outline of what these expeditions can all too often be like. But I have yet to describe the sort of people who go on them.

Of course, there are the honest, genuine hunters, guides who make it a point of honour to bring their clients up to the quarry in accordance with the rules and to provide them with opportunities to shoot but only in accordance with the basic laws of respect for life. Unfortunately there are others for whom the only laws are the laws of business and the only rule to please at all costs the customer who pays them. "The customer is always right", they say, just like the manager of a bistrot, and they are prepared to do anything to please their clients in the hope that they will come back again. Like sound tradesmen they honour their contract by arranging for their client to kill a lion, an elephant or an antelope—but just consider the way they go about this.

Having pocketed the price of the trip—out of which, of course, they take their cut—as well as the "expenses" which enable them to pay for the upkeep of their Landrovers and the wages of their local collaborators, the cash for daily meals and for the comfortable tents in which the party is housed, they have to "deliver the goods" in return. So in exchange they "guarantee" not only the game they have located, which their customers will slaughter with the greatest equanimity and under the most favourable conditions, but also the certainty of being photographed posed beside the carcass of some large beast and thus of going down to posterity to the acclamations of an admiring family and suitably impress-ed friends. Of course, these merchants are obliged to deal with simpletons and blunderers and have to succeed in fulfilling what can only be described as their part of the bargain. They are no better than more conventional gangsters and robbers who exploit the simple-minded and —though in this case they do run some risk—attack banks or even solitary old ladies. At times, however, the latter manage to ward off their attackers. This is more than can be done by an antelope fired at from a jeep by a rich man's girl friend who has never held a rifle before and who, when her bullet wounds but does not kill, never bothers to seek out the wounded victim but leaves it to a lingering ten-day agony in the savanna.

If Daumier had known of this "industry" it would have aroused his utter disgust and inspired his vengeful artistry.

In one short life one cannot hope to cover all the quirks, the vices and the cruelties of creatures that refer to themselves as human and who are astonished when one points out the inhumanity of destroying, on unequal terms, animals created to live a life of freedom and not to be murdered in this cowardly fashion.

How I regret that the man whose first name—Honoré—became him so well is no longer alive to devote his talent and the energy aroused by his indignation to an all-out attack on some of the hunters of today. First of all, to make us laugh at them by showing them to us for what they are, and to record their grotesque, pretentious image for generations to come. A record such as this would provide much food for thought, would enlighten, educate and serve as a warning against the facile, cowardly approach that is, unfortunately, all too common in hunting today. For these are merely the inevitable reflection of a society which, unless it undergoes a profound change of heart, neither time nor what we like to call "civilization" can save from shipwreck and extinction.

Paul VIALAR

A translation of each caption is given before the notes

to the individual plates

CHASSE ET PÊCHE,

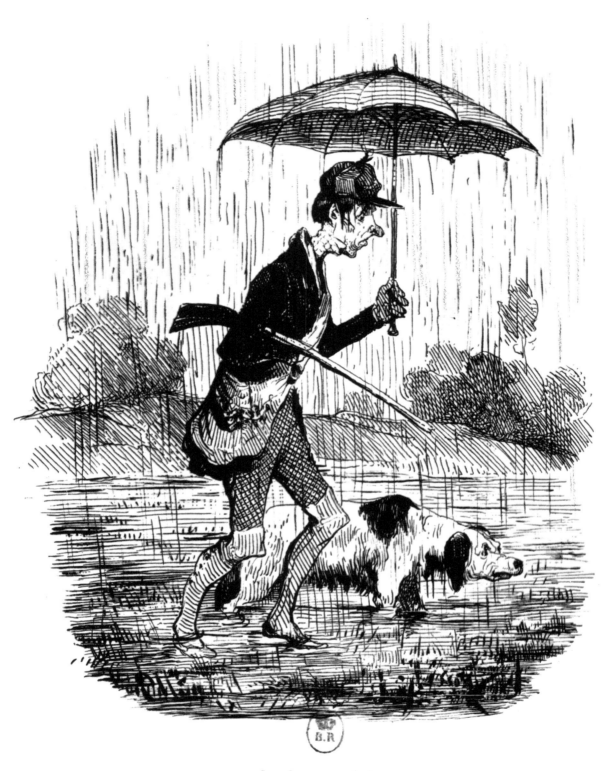

La chasse en Automne

LES PLAISIRS DE LA CHASSE .

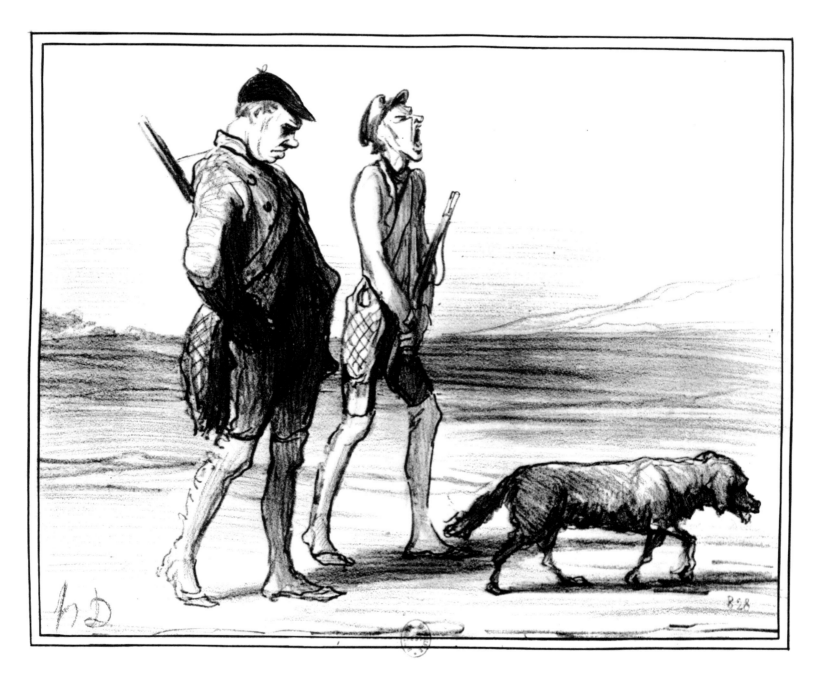

– Voilà pourtant ce qu'on est convenu d'appeler les vives émotions de la chasse!....

ÉMOTIONS DE CHASSE .

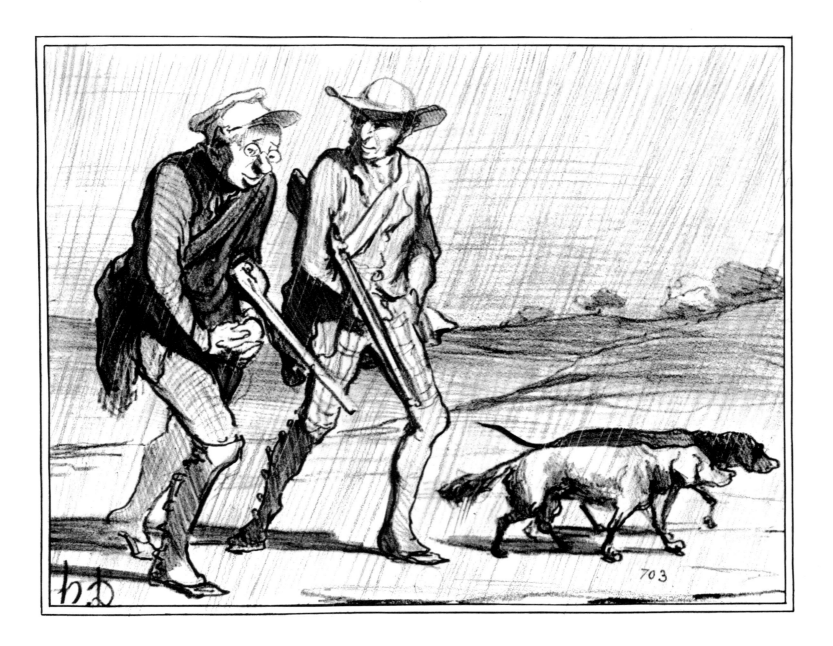

— La pluie tombe déjà comme ça depuis plus d'une heure et ça n'a pas l'air de vouloir cesser, je commence à craindre que nous ne finissions par être mouillés.

ÉMOTIONS DE CHASSE

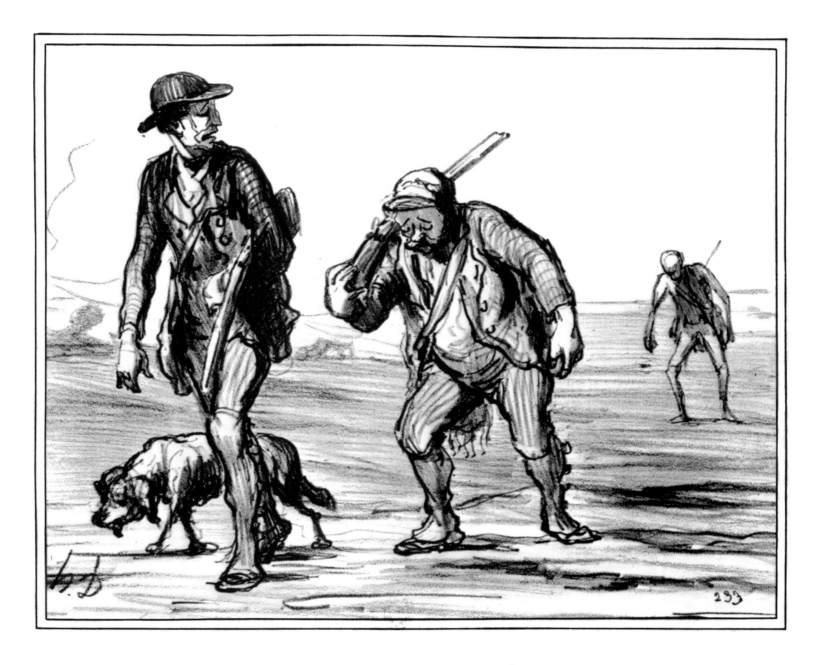

– Allons, m'sieu Pomard.... un peu de courage ....nous n'avons plus que deux lieues à faire et nous nous reposerons ....
– Quelle chance que nous n'ayons rien tué....je n'aurais jamais eu la force de rapporter un perdreau !....

ÉMOTIONS DE CHASSE .

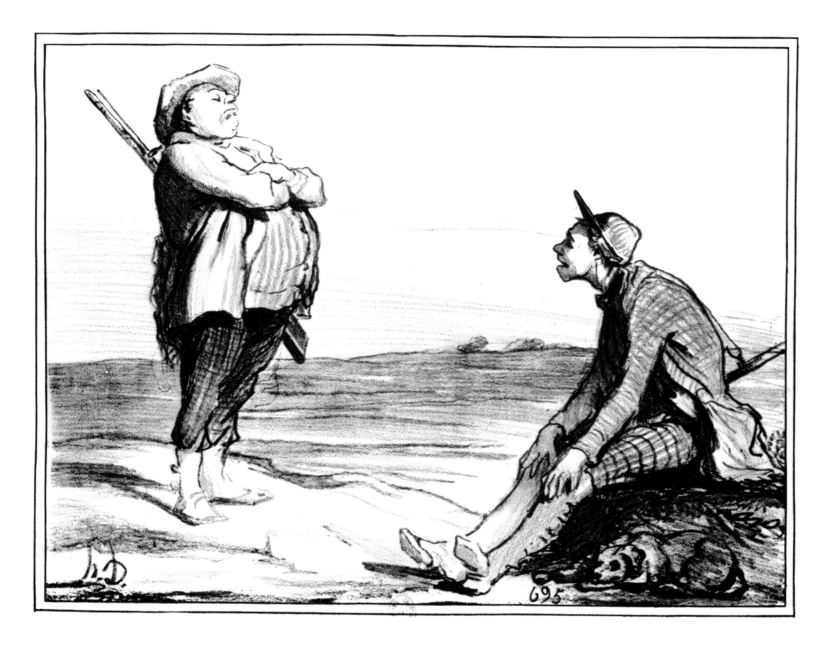

– Eh! bien , que faites-vous là, monsieur Crunichon?.... ce n'est pas en restant assis sur ce gazon que vous comptez tuer quelque chose, je pense ?.......
– Mais, si fait, si fait,... je me place commodément pour mieux tuer le temps ....

ÉMOTIONS DE CHASSE.

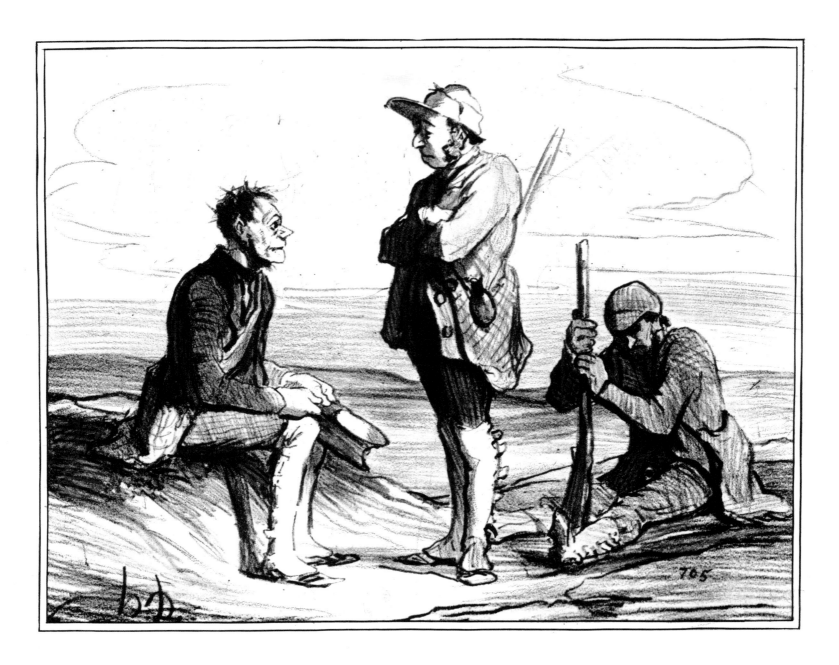

— C'est bien décidé..., je ne chasserai plus avec vous!....
— Et pourquoi cela ?.....
— Mon cher ami , vous êtes trop laid, vous effrayez le gibier !...

ÉMOTIONS DE CHASSE

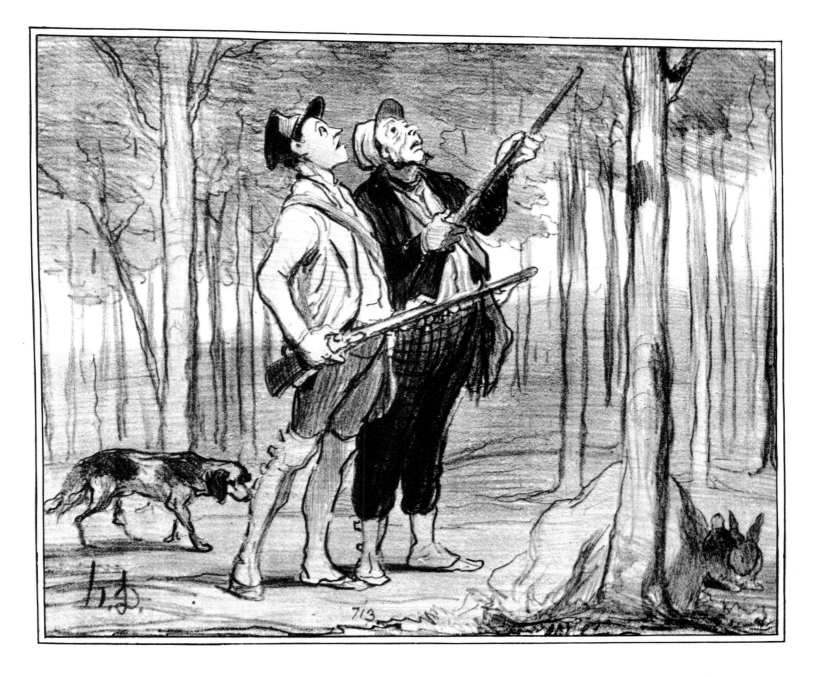

Je vois remuer quelque chose au sommet de cet arbre ...... ne serait-ce pas notre lapin qui aurait grimpé la-haut ?....

CROQUIS DE CHASSE.

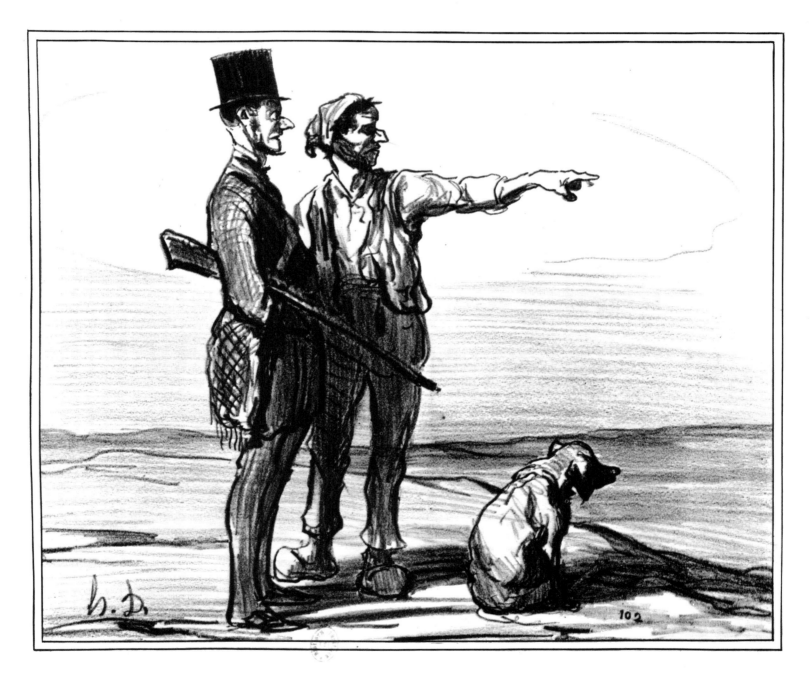

– Tenez.... j'avons vu un lièvre qu'aviont passé par là ......
– Est-ce qu'il y a longtemps ?.....
– Nenni point....... n'y a pas pùs d'trois mois !......

PASTORALES.

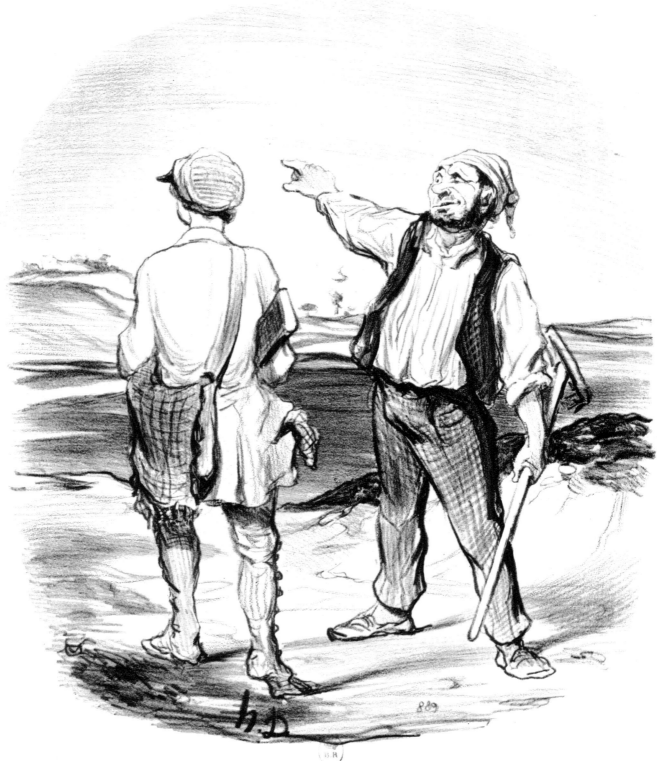

– J'ai vu un lièvre d'l'autre côté d'la ferme.... (**à part**) il y a huit jours !....

CROQUIS DE CHASSE

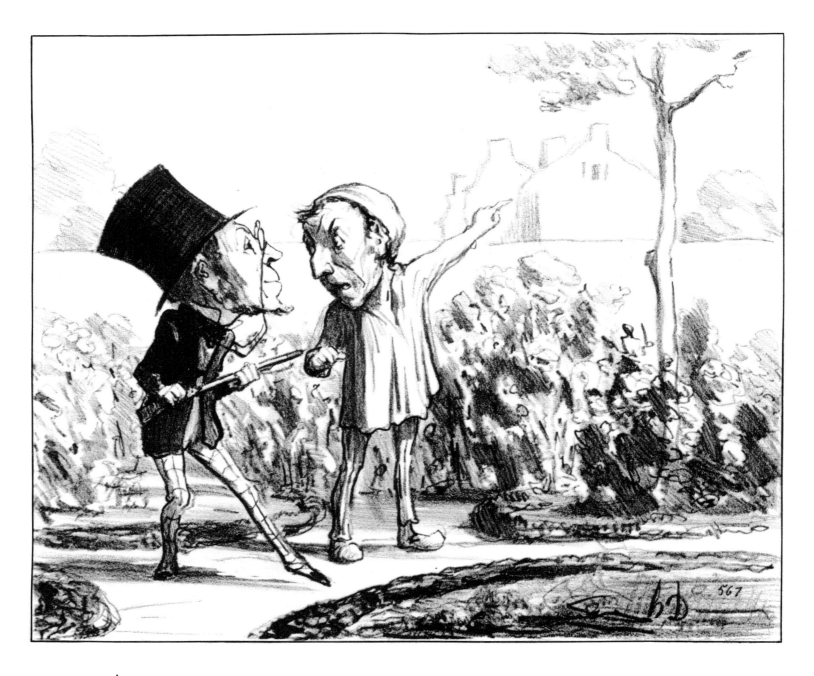

—T'nez not' Maîtr' en voila un p'tit qui mangiont toutes les r'coltes du pays, flanquez y un grand coup d'fusil!..
—Je crois que c'est un faisan!..

CROQUIS DE CHASSE

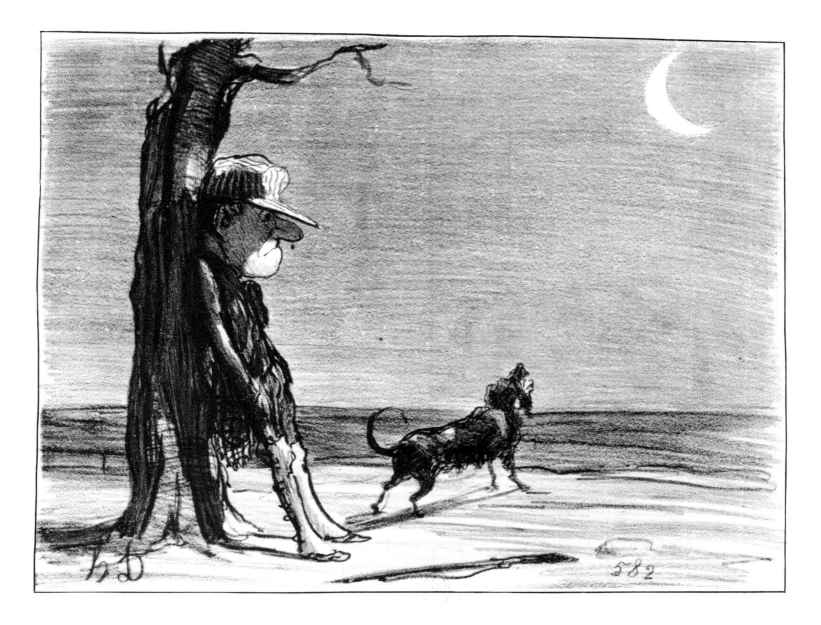

— Quelle fichue idée j'ai eu de venir chasser dans ces satanées plaines de la Sologne sans bien connaitre le pays ... pas moyen de trouver une ferme, me voilà obligé de passer toute la nuit à la belle étoile ... vais-je m'enuyer!. au moins mon chien passe son temps à aboyer à lune ca l'occupe!...

CROQUIS DE CHASSE

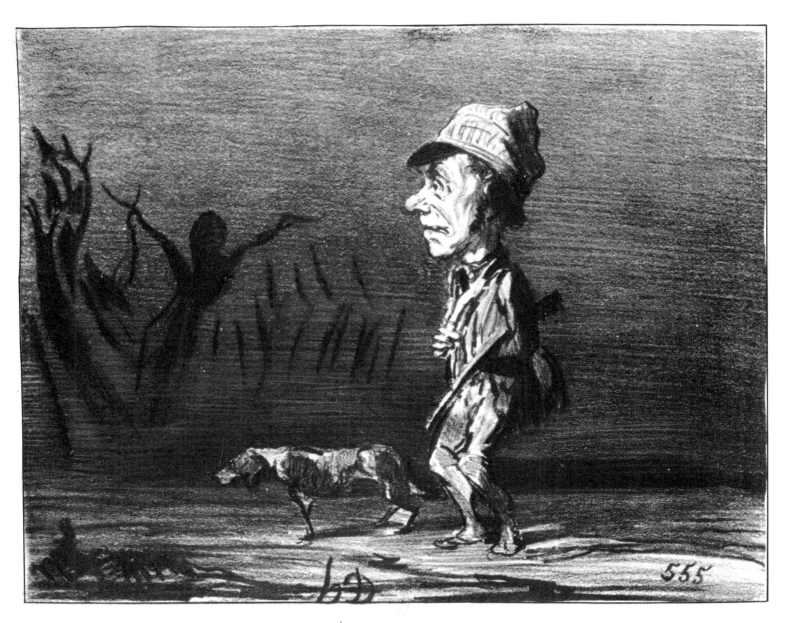

UNE ÉMOTION NOCTURNE

Mon dieu que j'suis donc fâché d'avoir poursuivi ces lapins si loin et d'rentrer si tard . . . c'est y un homme . . . c'est y un arbre . . . j'crois que c'est deux hommes .

CROQUIS DE CHASSE

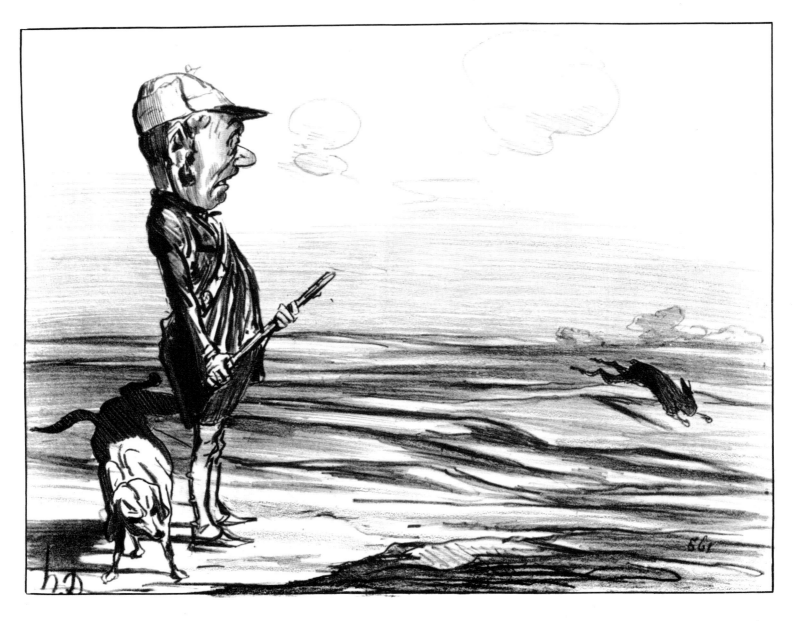

UN CHASSEUR NOVICE

— Je crois que c'est un lièvre ... comment diable ça se tire-t-il ? ...

ÉMOTIONS DE CHASSE.

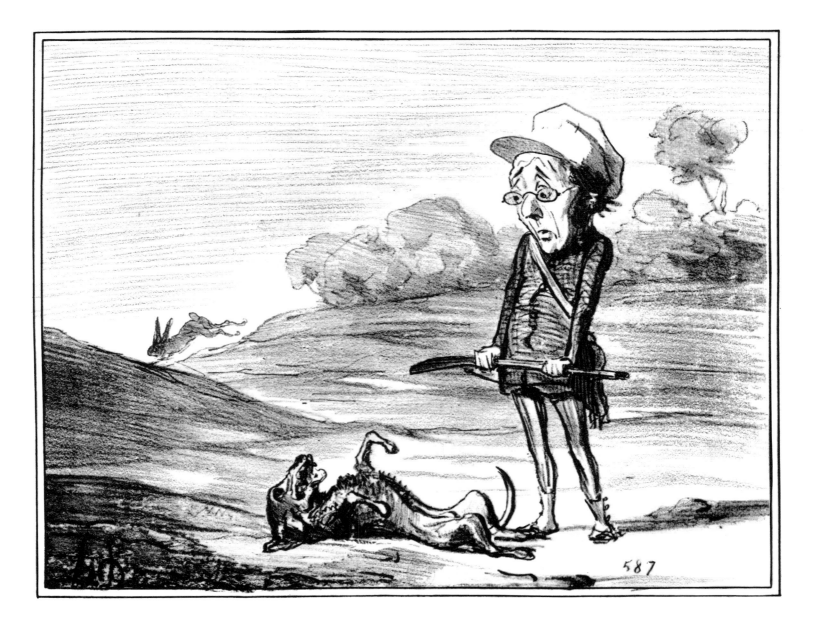

On dit que le chien est ami de l'homme , mais l'homme est il toujours bien réellement l'ami du chien ?...

CROQUIS DE CHASSE

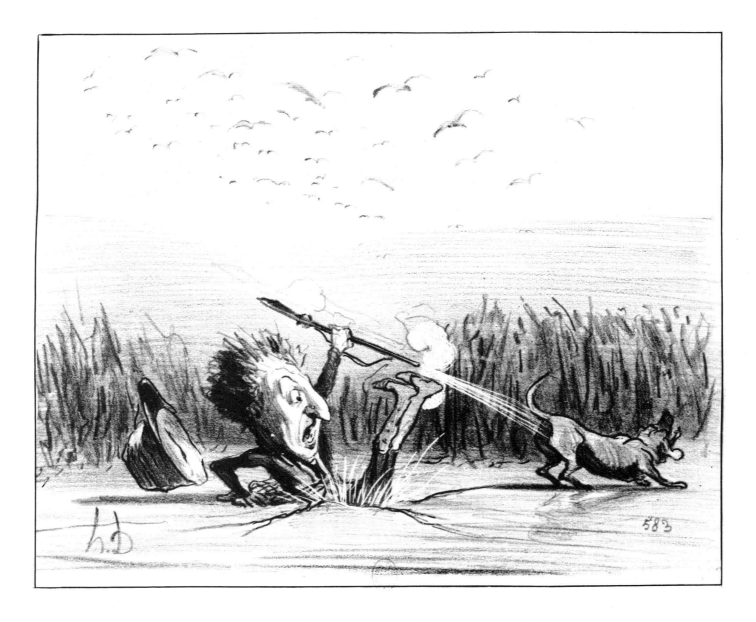

Un chasseur qui a du guignon et un chien qui n'a pas de chance.

CROQUIS DE CHASSE

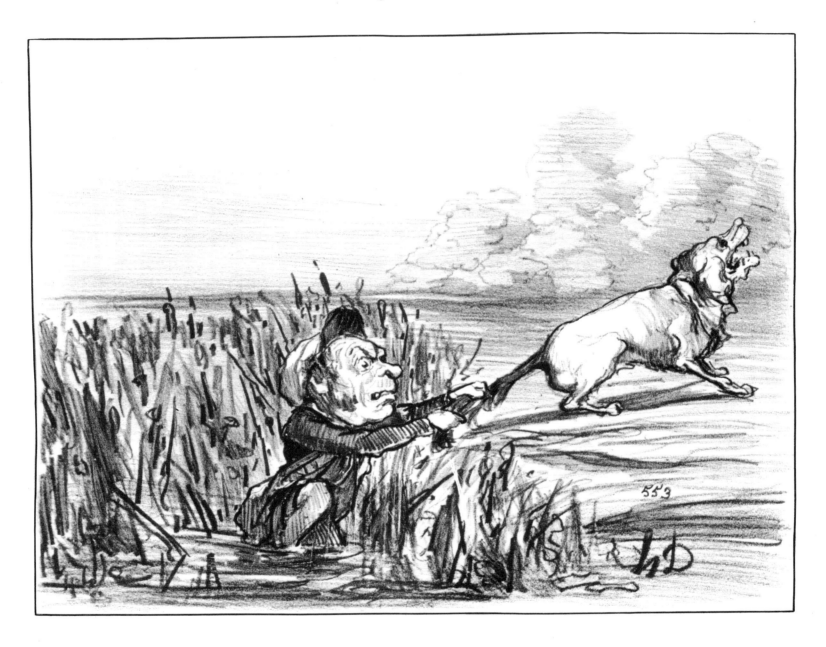

Ce qui nous prouve l'utilité d'avoir un epagneul quand on aime à aller a la Chasse au Marais.

CROQUIS DE CHASSE.

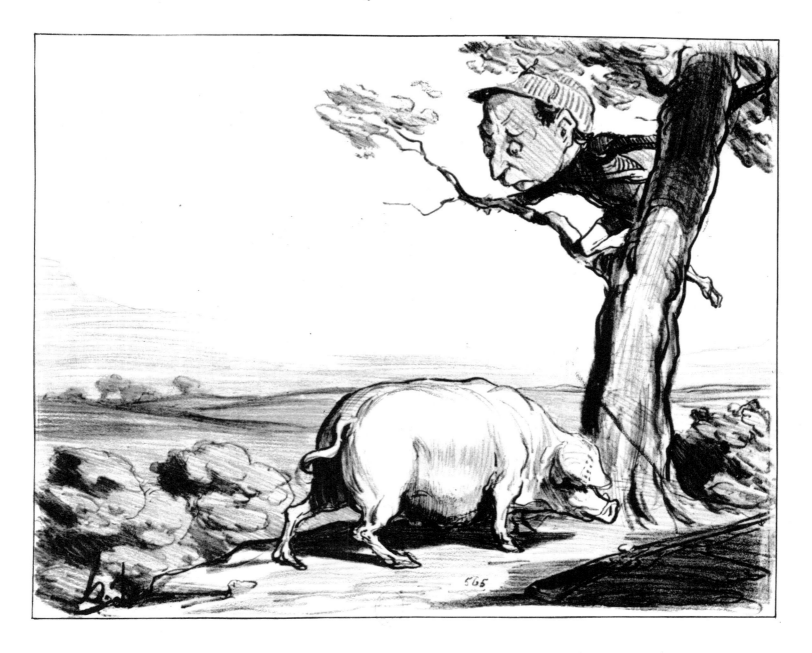

— Quelle affreuse Chose que d'avoir fait la rencontre de ce San lier... sans cet arbre j'étais perdu... il a l'air de réfléchir... puisse-t-il penser a s'en aller.

CROQUIS DE CHASSE.

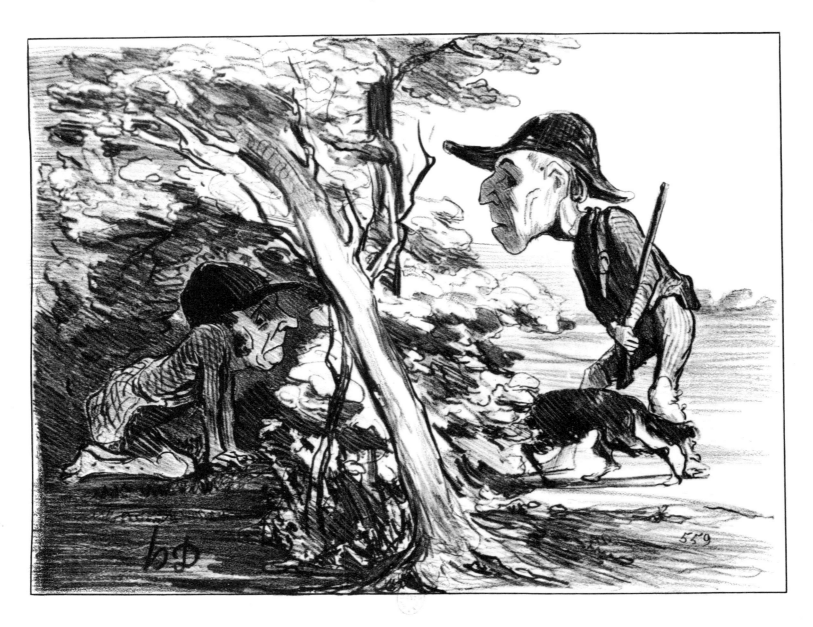

Dépisté!

CROQUIS DE CHASSE

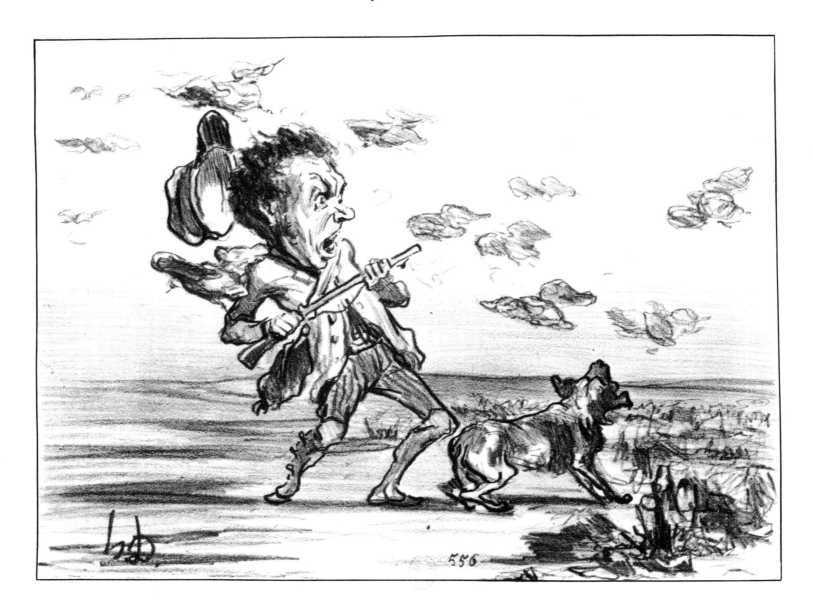

Inconvénient de chasser dans un pays où il y a trop de gibier.

ÉMOTIONS DE CHASSE

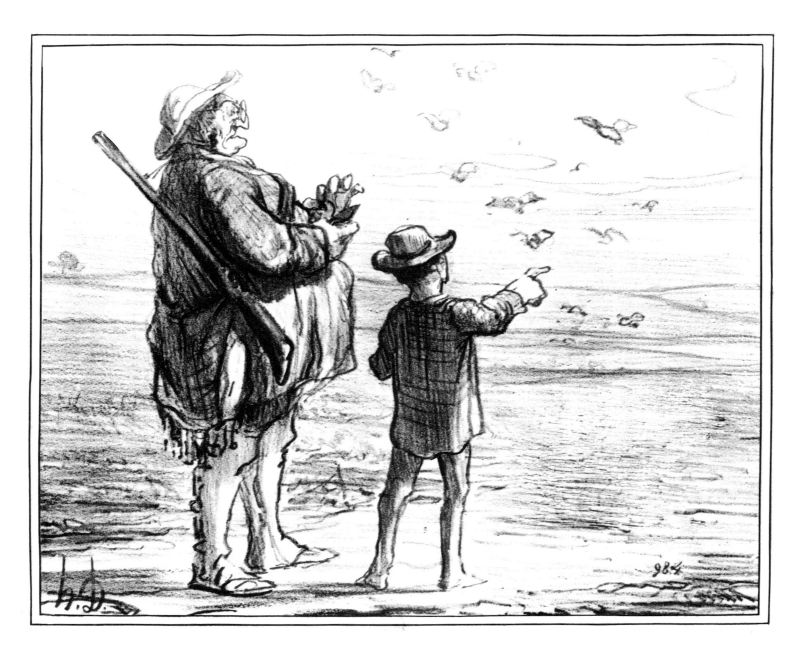

Mr PRUDHOMME À LA CHASSE.

– Ah! papa .... des perdreaux ...... tire dessus !.....
– Non, mon fils..... si nous tuons les perdreaux cette année-ci , nous n'en aurons pas l'année prochaine .

ÉMOTIONS DE CHASSE

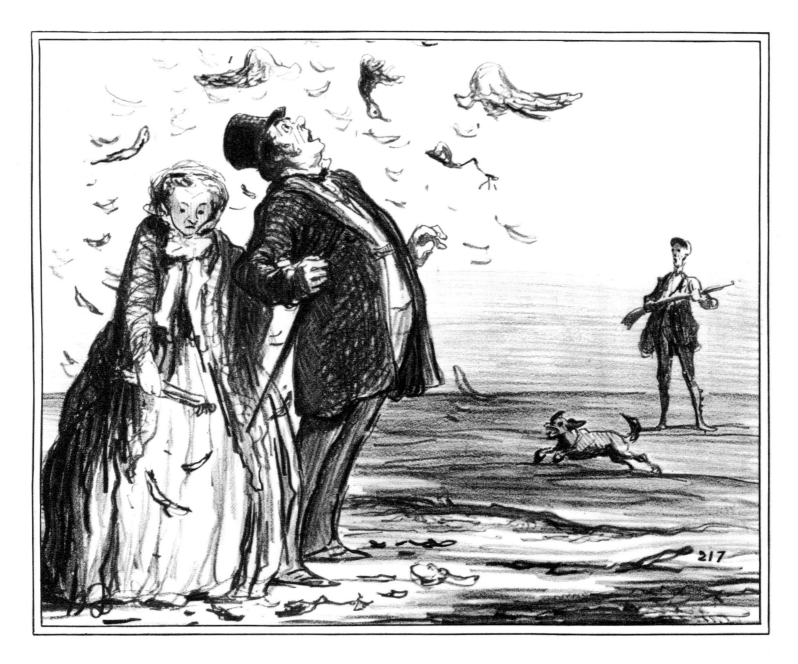

Inconvénient de tirer les perdreaux avec les nouvelles balles foudroyantes de Devisme.

LES BONS BOURGEOIS.

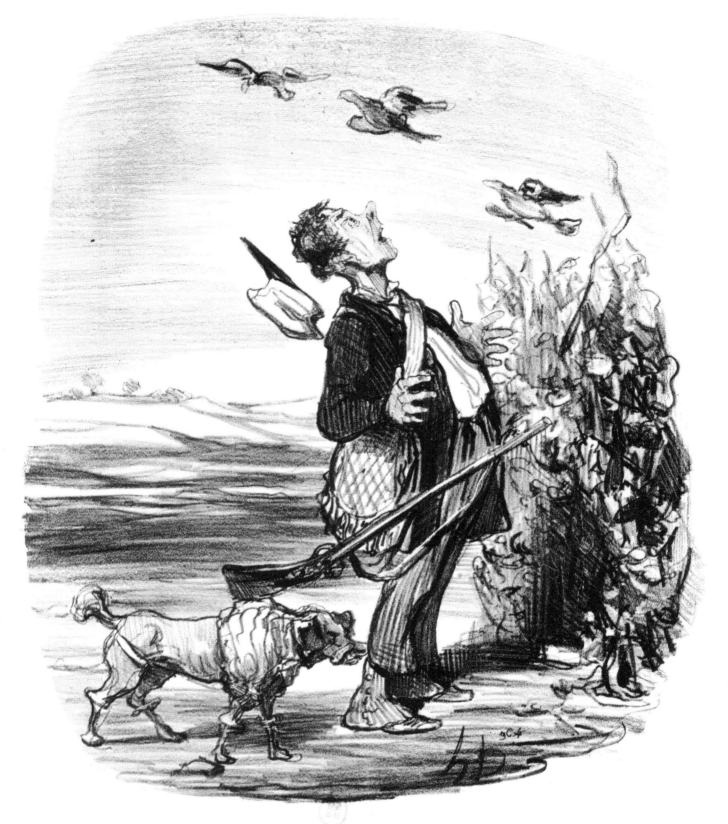

— Ah! sapristi....je crois que ce sont des oiseaux de proie..... ils mangeaient du raisin!..

QUAND ON A DU GUIGNON.

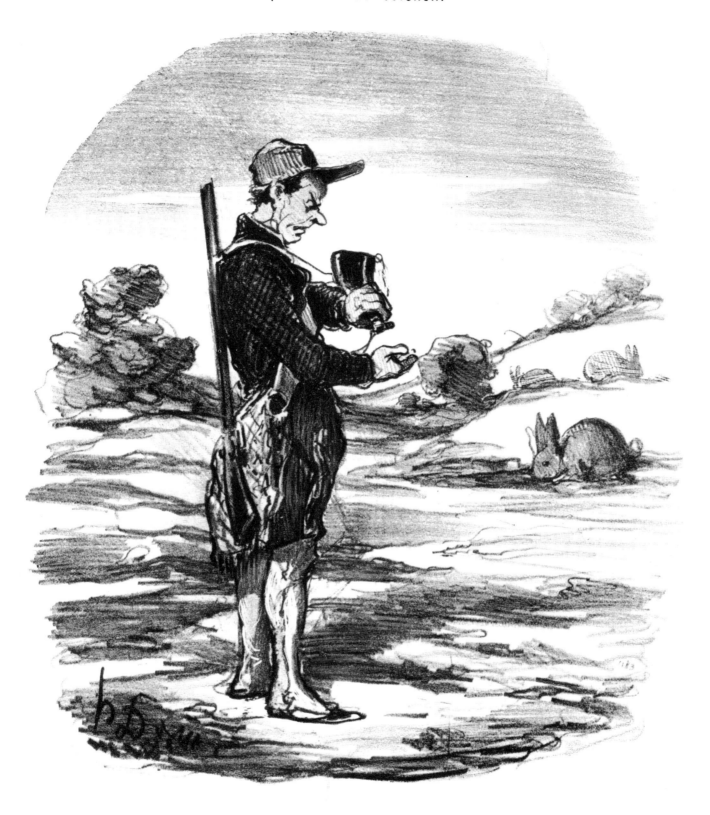

Et plus un grain de poudre !....

PASTORALES.

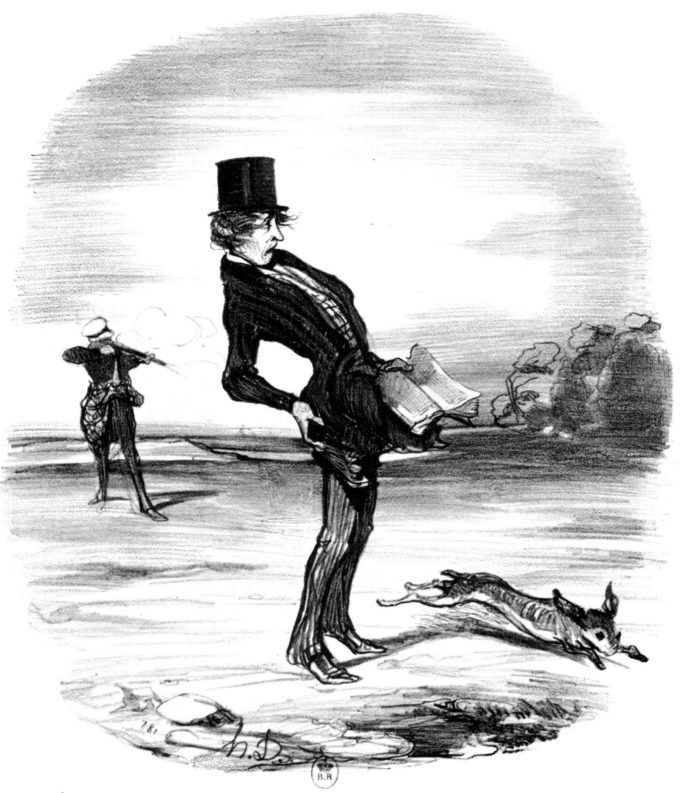

Comme quoi, au milieu du calme des champs, l'on peut éprouver tout-à-coup une vive émotion.

ÉMOTIONS DE CHASSE

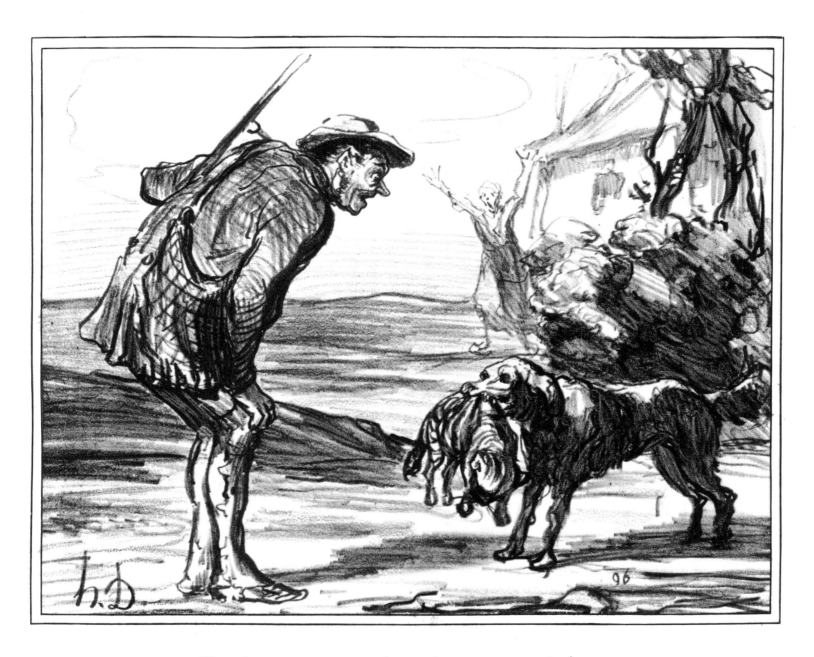

Tiens!....moi, qui croyais avoir tué un lapin!....

CROQUIS DE CHASSE

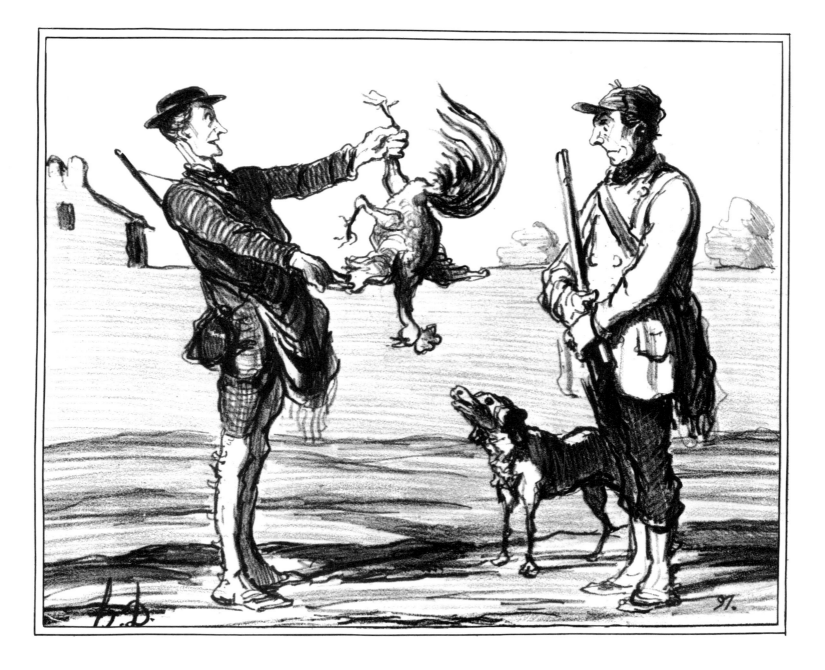

— Tenez, je viens de tuer un magnifique coq de bruyère !....
— Mais, malheureux !....c'est le coq Brahma de la ferme voisine...., un coq qui vous coûtera peutêtre plus de trente francs ....sans compter les coups de fourche !....

CROQUIS DE CHASSE .

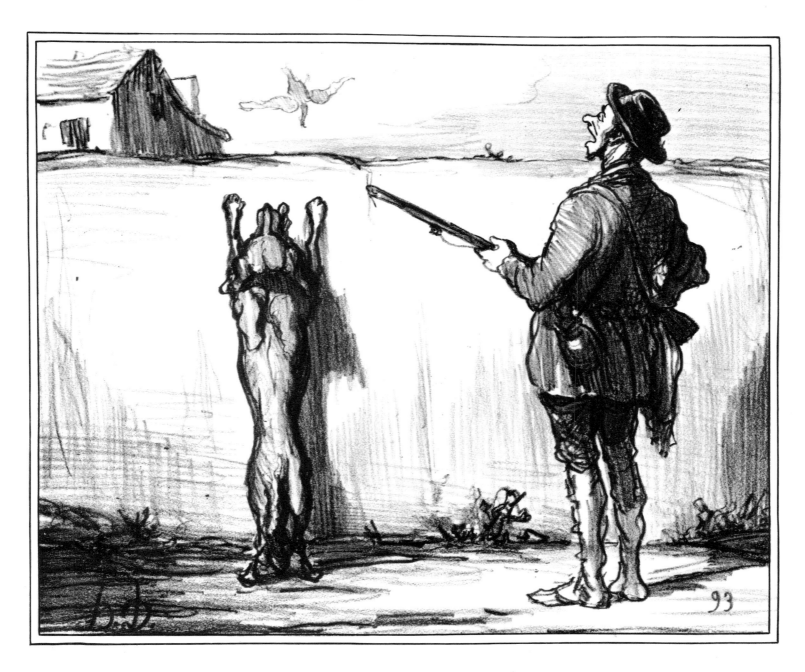

_ Allons, bon!.....pour un perdreau que je tue....., voilà qu'il tombe chez le voisin !.....

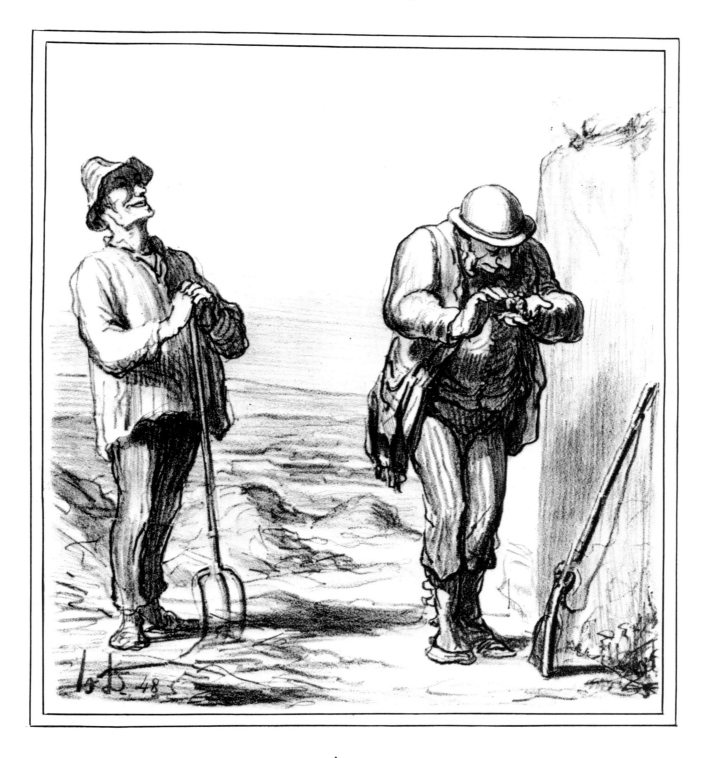

_ J'ai donc tué un Perdreau!....tiens c'est un moineau!...

29

ÉMOTIONS DE CHASSE.

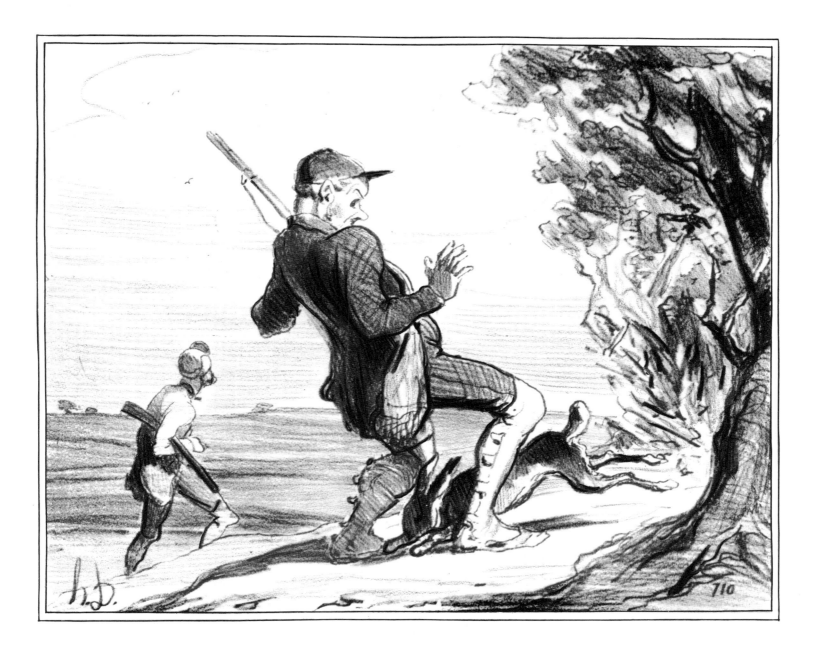

— Faut-il qu'un animal soit bête, pour vous faire une peur pareille !.....

ÉMOTIONS DE CHASSE.

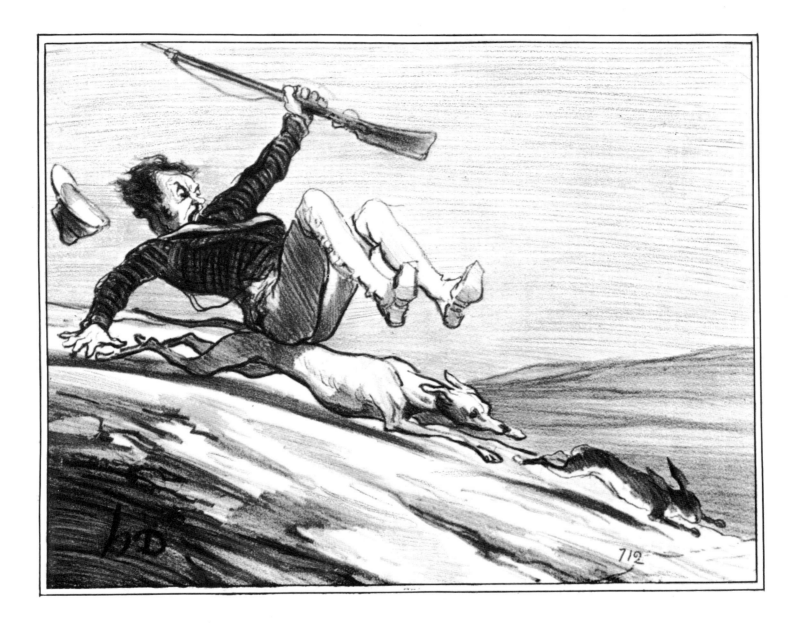

Comme quoi il n'est pas toujours agréable qu'un lièvre vous parte entre les jambes

ÉMOTIONS DE CHASSE

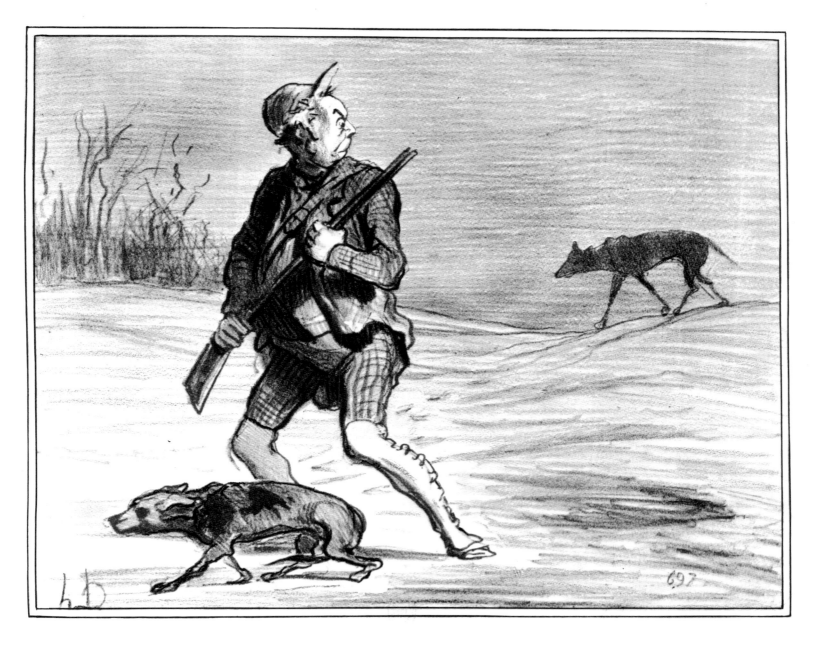

– Qu'est-ce qu'il a donc toujours à me suivre, cet animal..... je paierais volontiers six sous pour pouvoir monter dans un omnibus !..

CROQUIS DE CHASSE.

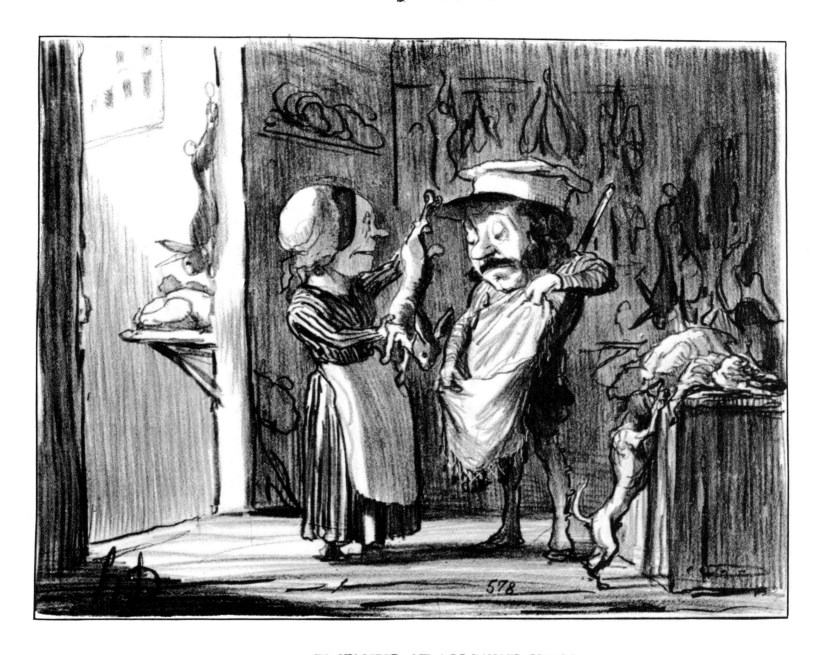

UN CHASSEUR QUI A DE L'AMOUR-PROPRE.

—V'la vot'affaire... fauty y joindre une belle oie?.. j'ai aussi un superbe homard!...

CROQUIS DE CHASSE PAR DAUMIER

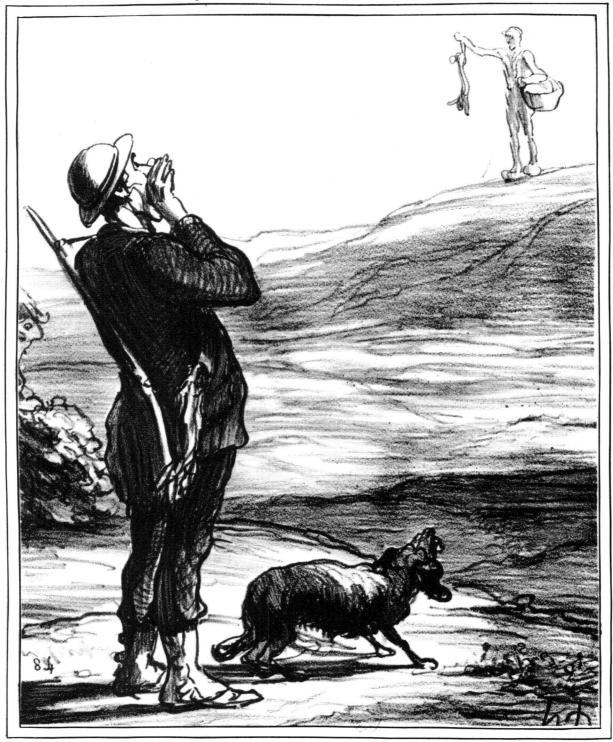

_ Ohé ! mon brave homme ! combien votre lièvre ?....
_ Quatre francs !
_ J'vous en donne cinq...mais tenez le comme ça et laissez moi tirer dessus !...

ÉMOTIONS DE CHASSE.

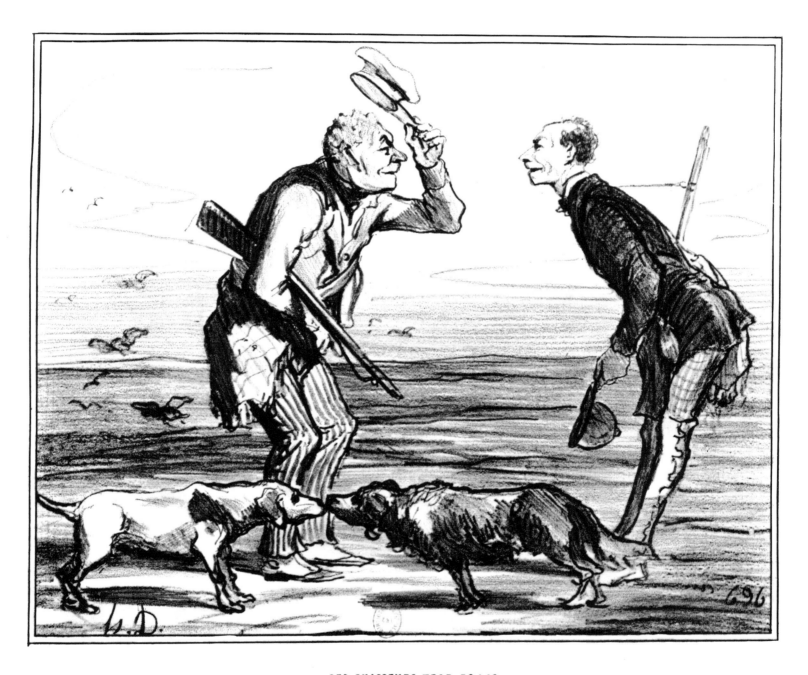

DES CHASSEURS TROP POLIS

– Madame Coquelet va bien?.... – vous êtes bien bon...... Madame votre tante ne souffre plus de son rhume de cerveau?.... – radicalement guérie....... et votre santé est toujours satisfaisante?..... etc²..... (Pendant ce temps)les perdreaux continuent à jouir également de la plus florissante santé.)

CROQUIS DE CHASSE

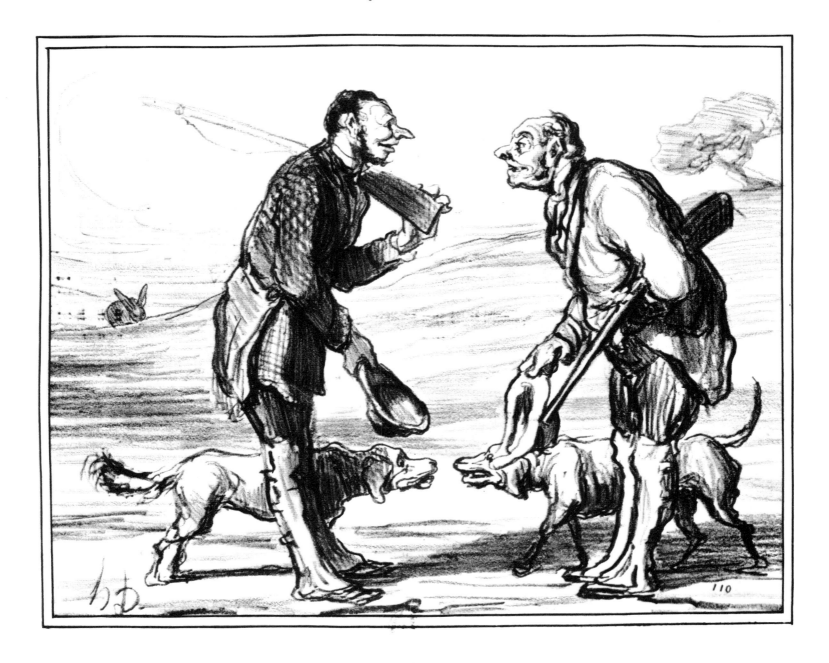

TROP DE POLITESSE

Tant que les chasseurs se demandent des nouvelles de leur santé les lièvres se portent à merveille....

(Aphorisme de S.t Hubert)

CROQUIS D'AUTOMNE par DAUMIER

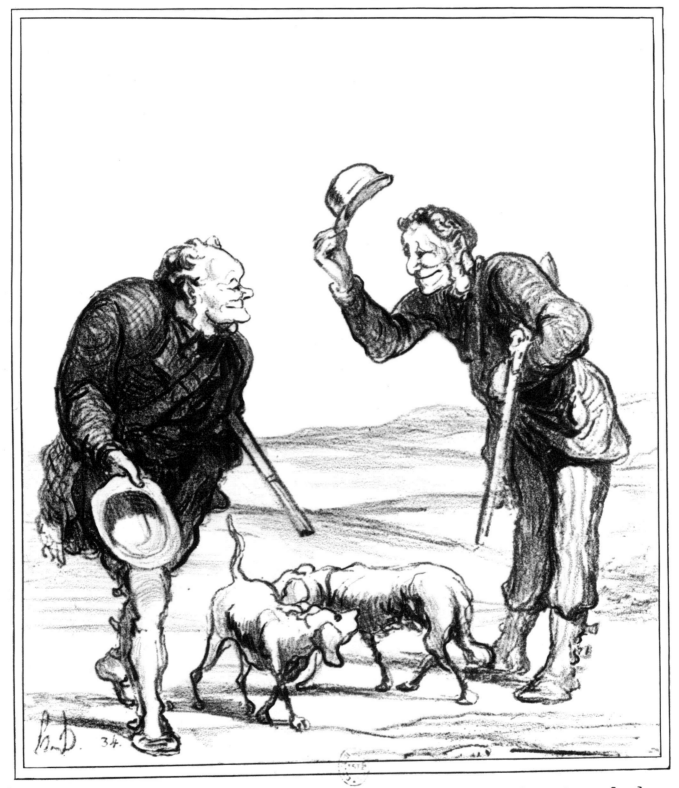

– Monsieur, vu l'absence complète de gibier je vous prie de vouloir bien m'accorder la permission de tirer sur votre chien.
– Monsieur, j'allais vous faire la même proposition! ...

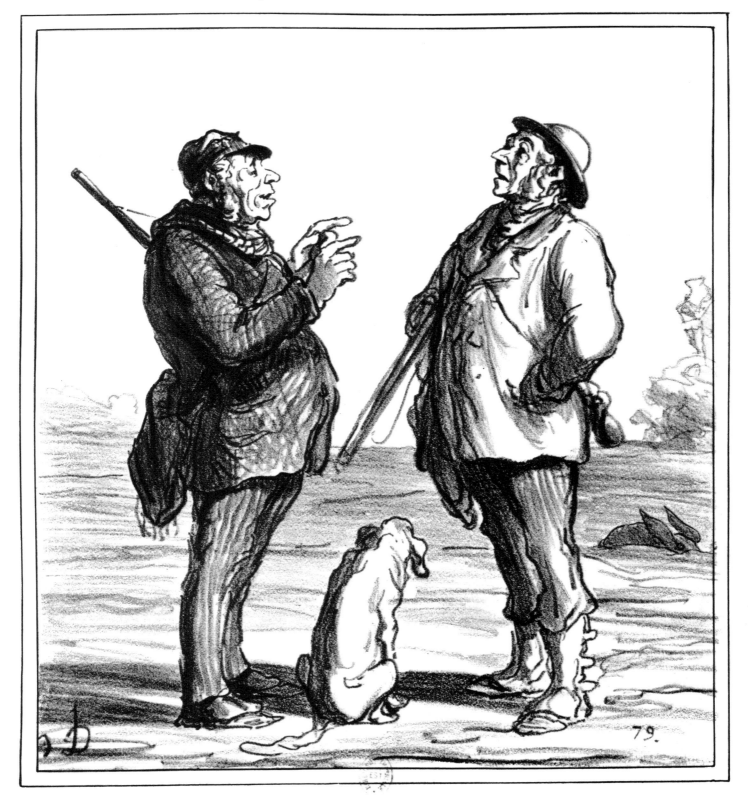

CROQUIS DE CHASSE. PAR DAUMIER.

— Moi d'abord sitôt que je vois un lièvre il peut se dire qu'il est mort ... et mon chien, quel flair !...

CROQUIS DE CHASSE PAR DAUMIER

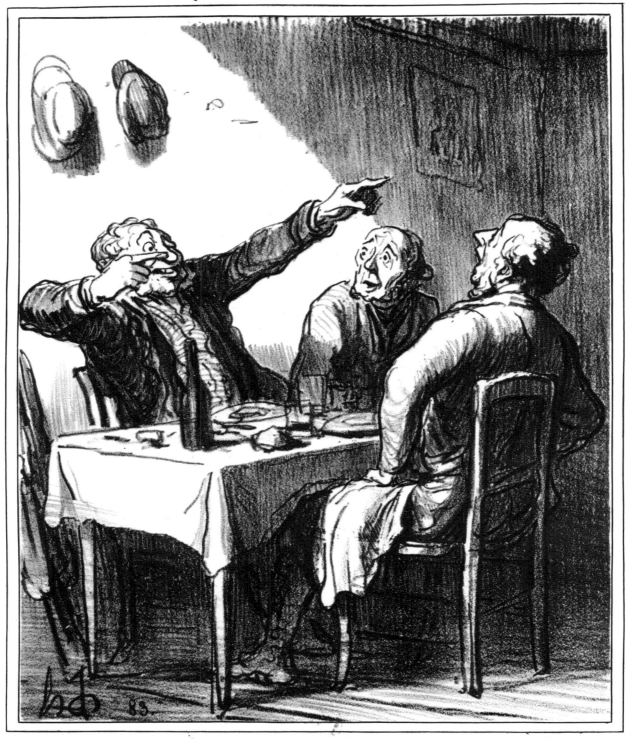

UN RÉCIT DE CHASSE

LE CHASSEUR.— Dans la même minute un lièvre part à ma droite ....pan! je le tue...le coup
de fusil fait lever à ma gauche une compnie de perdreaux ....pan! j'en abats trois!...
au dessus de ma tête passe un canard sauvage ....pan! il tombe.

UN AUDITEUR *(à part)*.— Ah! ça mais !....il a donc un fusil à trois coups !

CHASSE ET PÊCHE.

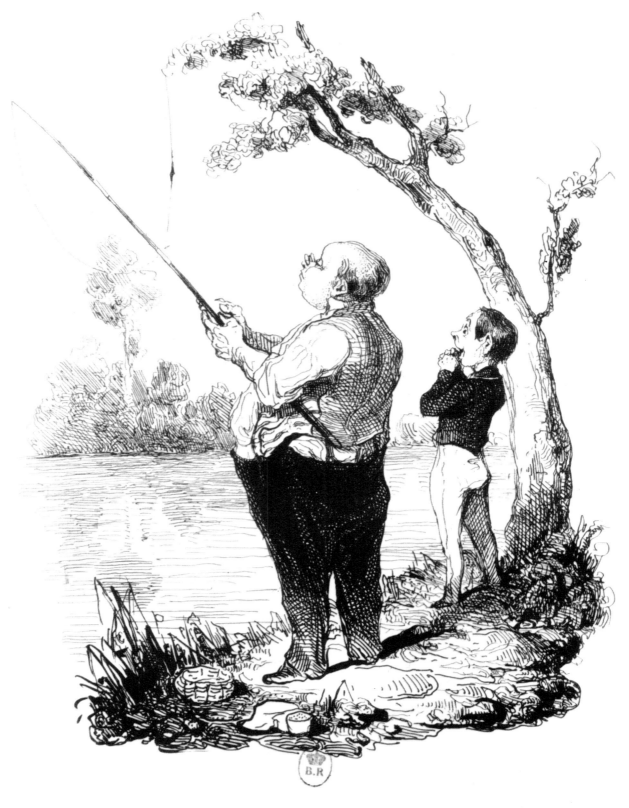

C'est drôle, voilà deux heures que le poisson ne mord pas!!

Cours d'histoire naturelle.

N.°2.

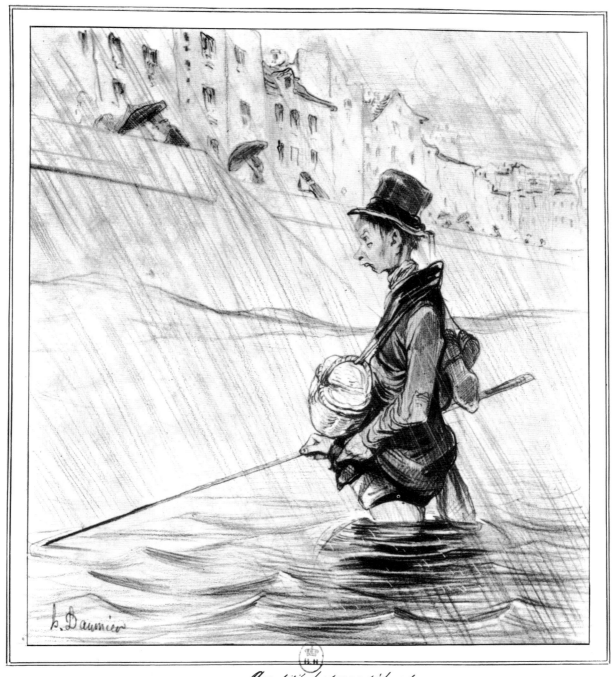

.....Ayez pitié du pauvre pêcheur!

Le Martin - pêcheur (our Seine)

Cette espèce de Martin-pêcheur ne pêche rien du tout. Au lieu de se plaire à voltiger et à poursuivre sa proie en zig-zag, le Martin pêcheur bipède reste immobile comme une borne aquatique, les bruits qui l'environnent, la pluie, la grêle, le tonnerre, les éclairs, les quolibets des passans, rien ne l'émeut, rien ne saurait le détourner de sa ligne. Quelquefois, après une journée entière d'attente il finit par sentir l'extrémité du roseau fléchir sous un poids inaccoutumé, son œil s'anime, son cœur bondit d'espoir et de bonheur, il tire avec précaution et ramène ... un vieux chausson ou une vieille savate, mais, à défaut de poissons il est toujours certain d'attraper des rhumatismes ou des fluxions de poitrine. Le Martin-pêcheur stationne d'ordinaire le long des quais par le froid, le vent et la pluie, enfoncé dans l'eau jusqu'à mi-corps, c'est ainsi qu'il descend gaiement le fleuve de la vie. Et lorsqu'enfin la mort vient le saisir, il se prend à douter de l'existence du goujon.

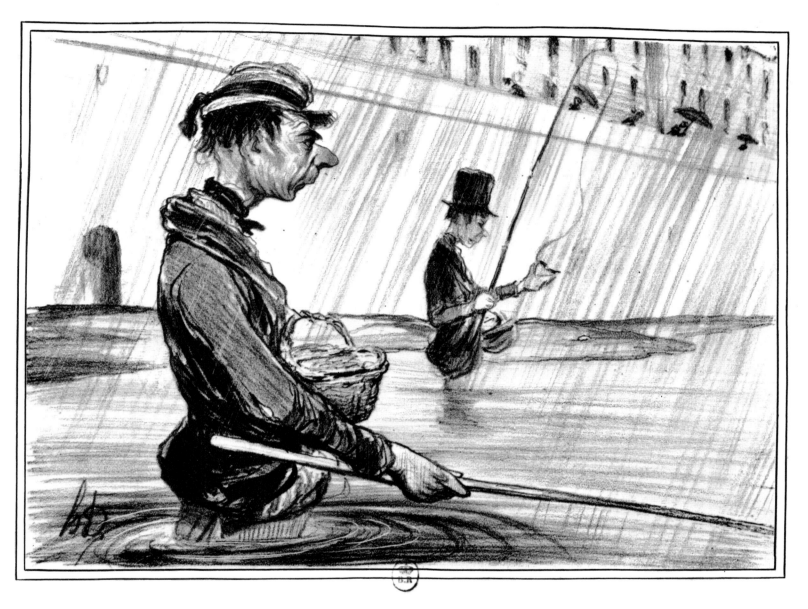

LE VIEUX PÊCHEUR.

Le pêcheur à la ligne est l'homme indépendant, persévérent et résigné, l'adversité ne le décourage pas, il combat tous les embarras qui l'entortillent; philosophe, il subit les orages et ne murmure jamais.

LES BONS BOURGEOIS.

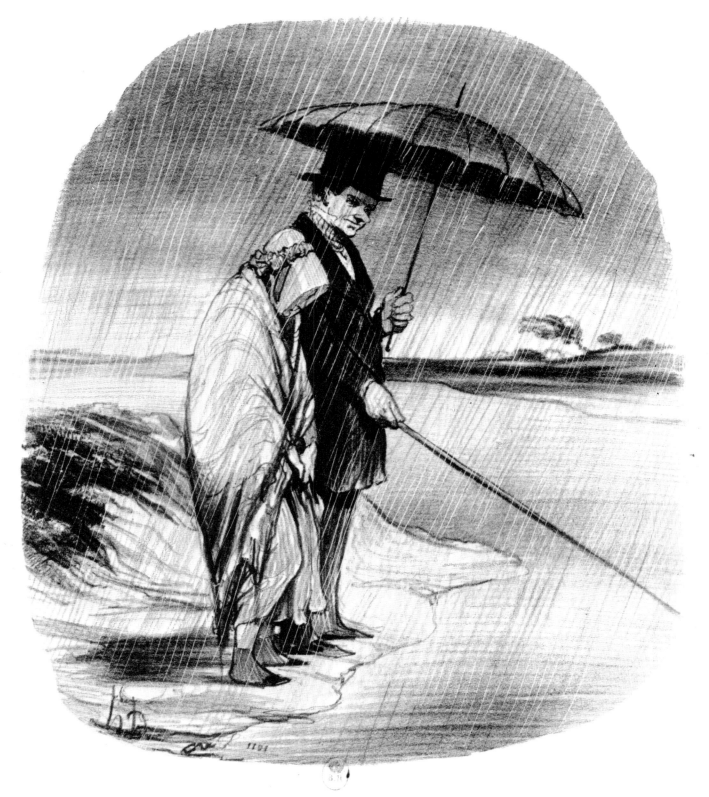

— Nous ne partirons donc pas !....
— Hortense je crois que ça va mordre...rien plus qu'une petite demie heure!...

TOUT CE QU'ON VOUDRA.

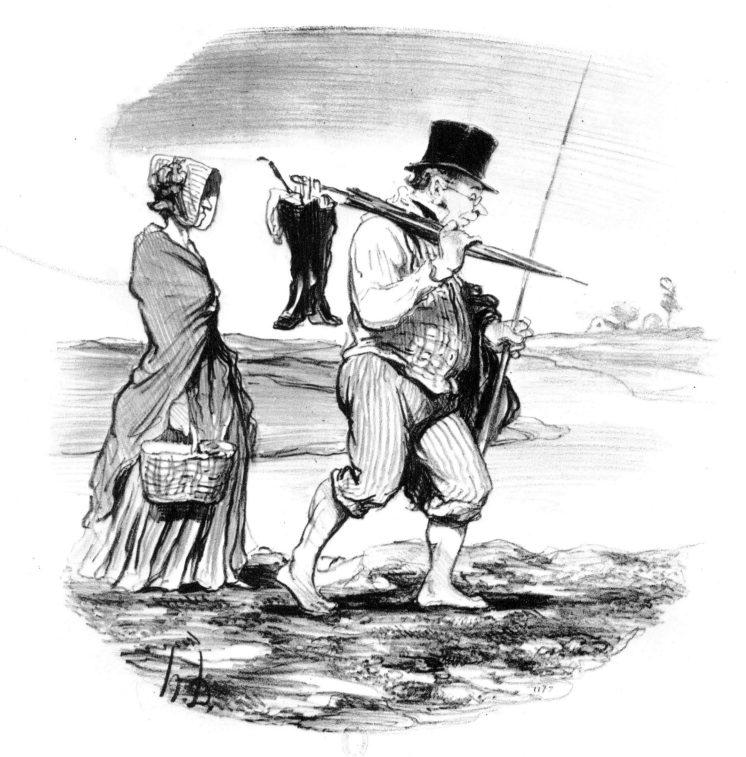

La femme, doit suivre, son mari partout ou il lui convient d'aller élire son domicile.

(Code civil titre du mariage)

LES BONS BOURGEOIS.

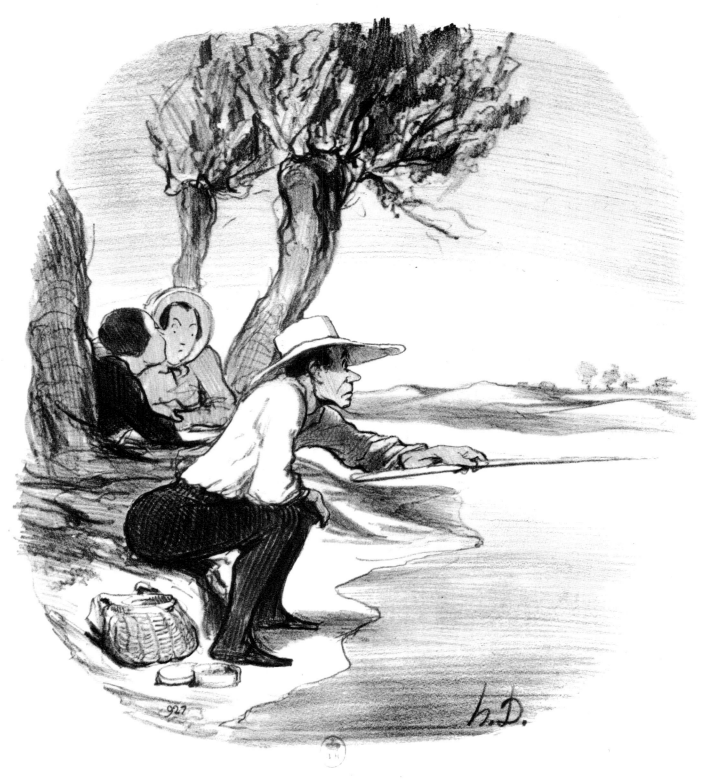

— Ma femme......ça mord.......ça mord !....

TOUT CE QU'ON VOUDRA.

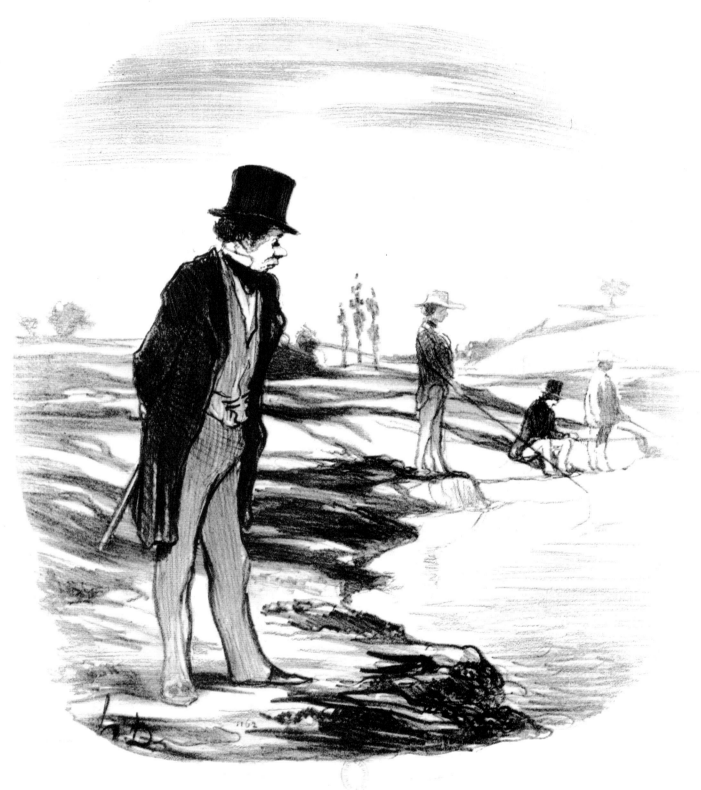

—Comment peuvent-ils trouver amusant de rester comme ça pendant quatre heures au bord de la rivière…
….moi au moins je joue aux dominos!……

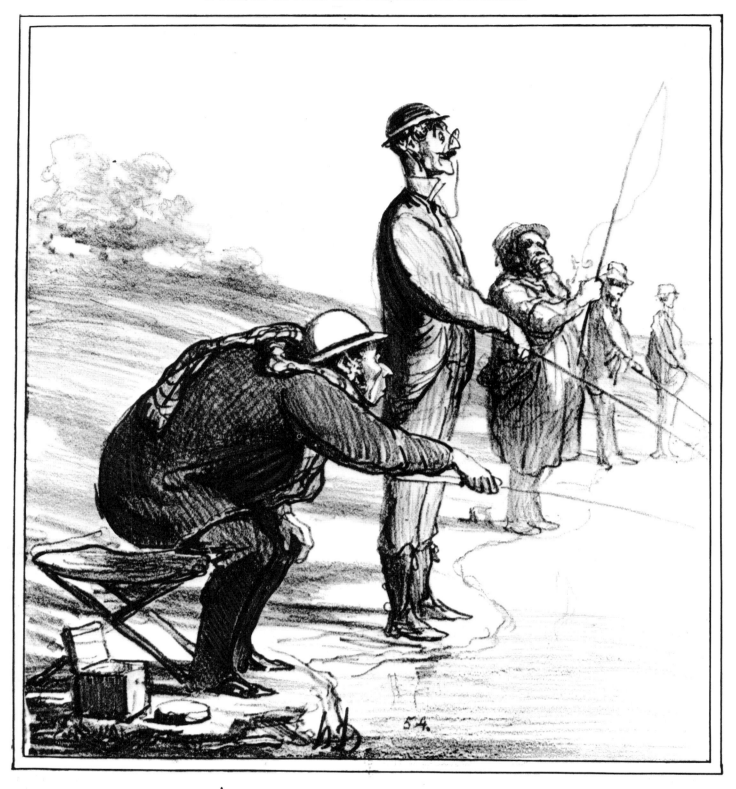

– Ça mord, quelle chance !
– Je vous défends d'attraper un poisson avant moi ; n'oubliez pas que je suis votre Vice-Président

TOUT CE QU'ON VOUDRA.

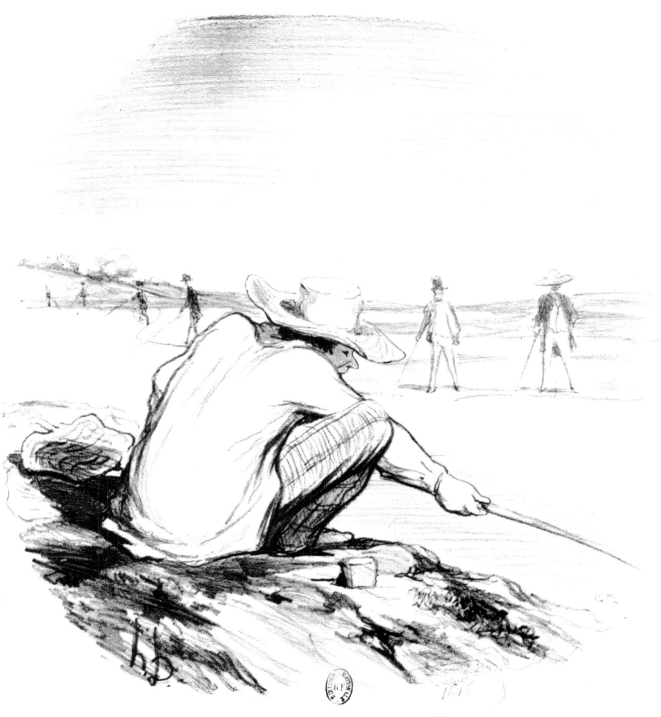

Aspect de la Seine de Paris à Chatou.

ACTUALITÉS.

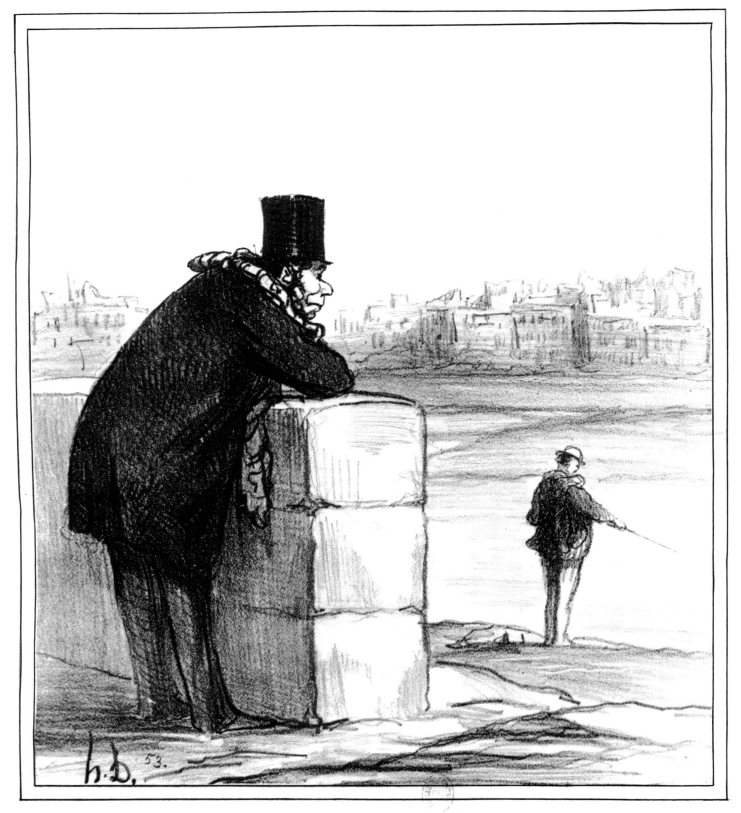

— Voici un monsieur qui vient pêcher tous les jours ici, depuis le matin jusqu'au soir;
je vais tâcher de connaître son adresse, et de savoir si sa femme est jolie.

If it is true, as Buffon asserts, that "the love of hunting, like the love of fishing, is natural to all men" **(Histoire Naturelle)**, *Daumier's contemporaries were no exception to the rule and furnished him with innumerable models for his drawings. As always when he depicts men, Daumier is less concerned with what they are doing than with what they are like. Hunting and fishing were no more for him than another pretext for poking fun at the middle-classes of his day, their idiosyncrasies, their stupidities and their pretentiousness. And this pretext was perhaps one of the best he ever found; it was certainly one of those that best inspired his hand. One of his contemporaries said that "nothing is more instructive than hunting; it is when they are in the midst of the woods, the fields, the meadows that one can best observe men, because the country air sweeps away the disguises with which they cover their faces in the cities".* (Physiologie du chasseur, 1841.) *Daumier, that tireless observer of the human race could not fail to exploit such a marvellous subject.*

The first caricatures on hunting and fishing date from 1836. This was not just a matter of chance; it was a consequence of the laws of 1835 which, by restricting the liberty of the press, forced Daumier to temper the violence and the number of his political attacks, and thus to find other subjects. But once he realized just how much he could make of these themes, imposed as they were both by a certain topicality and by orders from above, he set to work on them with all his enthusiasm and all his talent, to give us the masterpieces to be found in these pages. For his part, Arsène Alexandre considered that "the most remarkable episodes (from middle-class life of his day) are contained in the hunting and fishing series..., countless misadventures, as futile as they were painful, reproduced by a pitilessly accurate memory". *(Honoré Daumier, 1888.)*

These plates generally appeared at the opening and during the course of the hunting and fishing seasons. Some of them appeared on isolated occasions and others formed part of and rounded off series devoted to widely varying subjects: Cours d'Histoire Naturelle, Types Parisiens, Pastorales, Les Bons Bourgeois, Tout ce qu'on voudra, Quand on a du guignon. *But most of them were published in series such as* La chasse, Chasse et pêche, Croquis de chasse, Emotions de chasse, Les plaisirs de la chasse *and* Croquis d'automne. *Some of these titles were used several times for different series. Thus* Emotions de chasse *occurs twice, in 1854-55 (set of 15 plates) and in 1856-58 (22 plates);* Croquis de chasse *occurs four times, 1853 (21 plates), 1857-58 (4 plates), 1859 (7 plates) and 1864 (6 plates).*

Portrayals of hunting and fishing, whether humorous, decorative or documentary (fashion engravings), were plentiful in Daumier's day. Many of them were English, of course, but there were also French ones; numerous hunting Miscellanies *and* Sketches *took up the habitual subjects and the classic hunting jokes.* Hunting Memories *and the* Return from Hunting *dealt with the emptyhanded hunter, the marksman who kills his dog, who forgets his cartridges, etc...; charming lithographs after Carle Vernet (stag and fox-hunting) and Horace Vernet (wild-fowling and poaching), series of hunting scene engravings by Martinet, de Grenier, sometimes also reproduced on plates (they are exhibited side by side in the hunting museum at Gien); hunting subjects by Gihaut and Decamps, about 1829, caricatures by Elie de Beaumont, about 1849, by Cham and by Bertail in the* Journal pour rire *(1852), and* Plaisirs *et* désagréments de la chasse *(1859), in which everything always seems to go wrong, coloured comic books of the end of the 19th century, and many others.*

Like his contemporaries, Daumier took up the classic comic scenes.

In the texts I have consulted there is no indication of what contemporary opinion thought about Daumier's hunting and fishing drawings. But that keen hunting man Léon Bertrand sometimes waxed indignant (La Chasse et les chasseurs, 1862) and wanted to restore the reputation of "the true hunting man, so often and so unjustly slandered by the pens and crayons of our Grandville". By which he meant, by our caricaturists.

*It was again Léon Bertrand who, in commenting on the art Salon of 1837, expressed this opinion of the pictures of hunting: "One thing is certain, my friend, those people have never been hunting." (*Letter to M. Gustave F. on the exhibition of 1837, published in the* Journal des chasseurs, April 1837.)

Was Daumier himself a hunting or a fishing enthusiast? It seems unlikely to judge by his drawings; there is no indication in any of his caricatures that he might have found any pleasure or interest in either of these two activities. On the contrary, he considered them to be the height of boredom, an even more tedious way of passing the time than "a game of dominoes". (cf. plate 45.)

The plates reproduced in this book are a selection of the most meaningful of the scores of drawings on hunting and fishing themes that Daumier made.

It has been thought preferable to present them grouped according to subject matter rather than in chronological order, since several themes recur quite often at different periods. The main theme that emerges from this collection is boredom, *an incommensurate boredom, whether due to the weather (rain or oppressive heat), to the lack of game or fish, or to fatigue; then* ignorance *and* incompetence—*particularly where hunting is concerned—are the source of many a mishap, or give rise to all kinds of imaginary dangers; finally, Daumier's hunters usually return* emptyhanded, *which does not, however, prevent them from recounting the most stirring* hunting tales.

In the notes that follow some of the plates we shall take the opportunity of discussing a number of related subjects: Who were the hunters depicted by Daumier? Where did they hunt?—The dearth of game—The hunter's dress and equipment—The countryside—Daumier's drawing of game—Weapons—The game laws.

The two major themes are presented separately, first hunting, *and then* fishing.

In order to place these pictures in the context of the period, various contemporary writings have been consulted. One group of these are anecdotal rather than technical publications which were intended for the same reading public as the caricatures themselves. These are in the same spirit as Daumier's drawings and include: Les Physiologies, *1841,* (Physiologie du chasseur, *by Deyeux;* Physiologie du Parisien en Province, *by C. Marchal;* Physiologie du Bourgeois, *by Henry Monnier);* Les Français peints par eux-mêmes, Encyclopédie morale du XIXe siècle, *1840-42 (9 vols.), which dealt with the most varied subjects (*Le Chasseur, *by E. Blaze;* Le Bourgeois campagnard, *by F. Soulié;* Le Solognot, *by Félix Pyat;* Le garde-champêtre; Le pêcheur des bords de Seine, *by F. Brisset...),* etc.

The other works consulted are more directly concerned with hunting. First of all Le Journal des chasseurs, *a veritable encyclopedia of hunting, the first issue of which appeared in October 1836. It was founded by two great hunting men, Léon Bertrand and Joseph la Vallée, of whom E. Jullien wrote that they had "given a new impetus to the literature of the art of hunting". Among their collaborators were Deyeux, E. Blaze, Toussenel, the Marquis of Foudras—whose novels about hunting are famous—Chapus, the Comte d'Houdetot, Léonce de Curel, Louis Viardot... Then there are various books and* Treatises *on hunting and fishing, the details of which are given in the notes alongside the quotations taken from them. All these books are a mine of interesting and amusing information on hunting and fishing in the middle of the 19th century.*

Jacqueline ARMINGEAT

Notes

1. HUNTING IN AUTUMN.

L. Delteil 308, third state of four. Plate No. 7 of the series *La Chasse* (a series of 16 drawings published in *Le Charivari* from October 1836 to April 1837). Published in *Le Charivari,* 21 December, 1836 (2nd state).

This series was republished several times (up until 1845). Published first under the title *La Chasse* (1836, 2nd state), it became, in 1840, *Chasse et pêche* (3rd state). In the 4th state the title of the series was omitted and the caption was changed to become: *The Bourgeois of Paris hunting in the marshes at Enghien* (*L'Album Chaos*, plate No. 2).

The style of Daumier's earlier drawings of hunting and fishing comes as quite a surprise, being so different from his usual compositions (cf. also the first fishing drawing). The pen lithographs are, in fact, copies of caricatures by the English artist Robert Seymour (1800-1836). If we compare them with Seymour's *Humorous Sketches,* we are astonished to find that Daumier altered practically nothing except for a few details of dress which would have been too "English" for the French public. In this drawing, for example, the hunter wears a cap instead of a top hat. But the rest of drawing is identical—the stance of the man, the kind of dog, the countryside.

Cham also reproduced this hunting scene almost exactly (did he copy it from Seymour of from Daumier?). Only the dog is slightly different because, in order to shelter under the umbrella, he is shown walking between his master's legs (*Manuel des chasseurs,* 1861).

Since this series forms part of Daumier's work, and indeed was a great success in his day, drawings from it had to be included. But, clearly, these drawings—or rather copies—added little lustre to his name. It is only when he relies on his own imagination and talent that he emerges as the outstandingly great artist he undoubtedly was.

2. SO THIS IS WHAT IS CALLED THE HEADY EXCITEMENT OF THE CHASE!

L. Delteil 2723, second state of two. Plate No. 2 in the series *Les Plaisirs de la chasse* (a series of two drawings that appeared in *Le Charivari* in September 1855. Published on 27 September.

"Next to love, hunting is perhaps of all the pleasures of this wicked world the most praised and the most reviled. Plato called it a sport for the gods; St Augustin a savage amusement; Lycurgus recommended it to the Greeks; Moses forbade the Jews to practice it; Pliny affirmed that it gave birth to the monarchical state; Sallust wanted it to be left to the slaves; Buffon wanted to make it the privilege of heroes. Surely these contradictory opinions arise because, under one and the same name, each person is talking about something different?..." (*L'Hermite de la Chaussée d'Antin*, 1814 — *La partie de chasse.*)

Buffon, indeed, is categoric in his opinion: "Hunting is the only pastime that completely diverts the mind from business, the only relaxation that is not indolence, the only one that provides an intense pleasure, never becomes dull and with which one can never become sated."

And what did Daumier think about it? His views were doubtless very close to those expressed in *Les Français peints par eux-mêmes:* "The revolution of 1789 completely changed the French hunter; he no more resembles the hunter of earlier days than a millionaire grocer resembles the Duke of Buckingham or Marshal Richelieu" (*Le chasseur*, by Elzéar Blaze, 1841).

But why do these two men, in their irreproachably correct garb, go hunting? The scowl on one man's face, the yawn of the other, even the downcast gait of the dog, bear witness to their unutterable boredom. Do they go hunting because they have to, because it is the done thing, because they have nothing better to do, because it is "the only pastime their wives cannot share with them"? *(L'Hermite de la Chaussée d'Antin).* Or is it because "Roy Madus, Gaston Phoebus and all the old writers on hunting recommend hunting as an excellent means of avoiding idleness...; they want us to walk, to tire ourselves out to work up an appetite and to keep fit"? *(Le Chasseur).* Is it just to have the satisfaction of exercising their *shooting rights?* "From 1830, hunting ceased to be the prerogative of the aristocracy. Citizens and small landowners, with their pointers or their basset hounds, wanted to indulge in it. It became clear that the French are eminently a hunting nation... Today hunting has become a real craze." (*La chasse, son histoire, sa législation,* by Ernest Jullien, 1868). Perhaps they go hunting simply because, "of all Frenchmen, the bourgeois of Paris is the most enamoured of the country life, a love which he pushes to fanaticism. Shopkeeper and clerk, confined behind a counter or chained to a desk, pass the long hours dreaming of the countryside." (*Le Bourgeois campagnard,* by Frederick Soulié, 1841.)

Daumier's genius lies precisely in knowing how to demonstrate with such talent the gap that exists between dream and reality, "the special comic flavour that emerges from the contrast of intention and result".

3. IT HAS BEEN RAINING LIKE THIS FOR MORE THAN AN HOUR AND IT DOESN'T LOOK LIKE STOPPING. I AM AFRAID WE ARE GOING TO GET A TRIFLE DAMP.

L. Delteil 2607, second state of two. Plate No. 7 of the series *Emotions de chasse* (A series of 15 drawings that

appeared in *Le Charivari* from October 1854 to February 1855). Published towards the end of 1854.

Although these two hunters are walking faster and with a more purposeful manner than those in the previous drawing, this is due to the rain and not to any greater interest in hunting. The bordeom to be seen on their faces is just as acute.

The *Journal amusant* of 14 January 1860, tells of a luckless sportsman who "hunted on the plain of Saint-Denis for fifteen hours and caught nothing more than a cold in the head... no heady emotions for this Nimrod."

It seems surprising today to think of people hunting on the plain of Saint-Denis, but, in the middle of the XIXth century, owing to its proximity, it was one of the Parisian's favourite haunts for walking and shooting. In the satirical drawings of his *Emotions de chasse* (1857), Cham depicts *The opening of the hunting season on the plain of Saint-Denis.* He portrays an almost unspoilt countryside with several hunters and their dogs and a few rabbits.

In those days it was possible to hunt almost anywhere around Paris, after passing through the "barrières" or city gates.

The author of *Physiologie du chasseur* (1841) notes that although there had been "a lot of building on the outskirts (of Paris), there were still open plains where anyone could walk with a gun in his hand."

In an article on *The end of the hunting season* (*Journal des chasseurs*, March 1837), Léon Bertrand lists the following as being among the places where one could hunt: "The fields of Arcueil and Cachan, with their splendid large marshes,... from Grenelle to Sèvres,... Clamart,... the plain of Saint-Denis, where my dog caught two cats since there were no hares,... Saint-Germain and Marly,... Meudon."

4. COME, COME, MR. POMARD... KEEP YOUR SPIRITS UP... ONLY TWO MORE MILES AND WE CAN REST...
— WHAT A PIECE OF LUCK WE DIDN'T BAG ANYTHING... I WOULDN'T HAVE THE STRENGTH TO CARRY A PARTRIDGE.

L. Delteil 2895, second state of two. Plate 21 of the series *Emotions de chasse.* Although the title is the same, this is a different series from the one from which the previous plate was taken. This second series, consisting of twenty-two drawings three of which were not by Daumier, appeared in *Le Charivari* from November 1856 to November 1858). Published on 29 October 1858.

As well as the rain, another unpleasant factor of hunting was the oppressive heat of certain September days. Daumier captures this here in masterly fashion in the figures of the two novice hunters, worn out and heavy with fatigue, and even the dog, with head low and lolling tongue. The sun is at its highest point for the shadows of the hunters are very short. The light is so intense that the figure of the straggler is blurred, almost in "impressionist" style. "It is agony walking about on the plain," says *L'Hermite de la Chaussée d'Antin*; "well, never mind, we agreed to enjoy ourselves until four o'clock."

The character encouraging the others is not dressed as a gamekeeper, but he is obviously acting as guide to the other two men. Now, "when gamekeepers guide the hunter, they always do so with graceful felicity... conveying the conviction that, with a little trouble and hard work, they will lead the hunter to success; but, in fact, their deliberate aim is to safeguard the game". *(Physiologie du chasseur)*.

This perhaps is what "Mr. Pomard" is experiencing.

Already at the beginning of the xixth century, people were deploring the rarity or even the disappearance of game. "From 1825 to 1840, the amount of game in France underwent a wholesale reduction... a few species have already disappeared completely. The red partridge, for example, which was very common twenty years ago, is no longer to be found at all in a number of regions; the hare has disappeared from deforested areas and from regions where properties have been divided up". (Comte de Saint-Aignan, *Report to the Zoological Society*, in the Society's *Bulletin*, October 1865). His report concluded that this devastation was due primarily to poaching.

The *Journal des chasseurs* also raised its voice against "the odious practice of poaching". Many articles and publications of the period agreed that the poacher was the real enemy of game.

But there were other reasons for this depopulation, in particular the dividing up of large properties, since "each owner... exercises his hunting rights or makes them over to someone else... with disastrous consequences" (M. de Saint-Germain, speaking in the Senate, 7 March 1867).

Yet another reason was "The excessive ease with which anyone can go in for hunting; and (I deplore) this, not for any lordly or aristocratic reason or attitude, but because each day brings us nearer the imminent date when France will be entirely devoid of game; when even the wren will be as scarce as the stag in our forests." (B.H. Revoil, *Bourres de fusil*, 1865).

And this was written in the middle of the xixth century when only 155,000 hunting licences were issued, as compared with the two million of today!

Alexandre Dumas, who practiced both hunting and fishing, also bore witness to the scarcity of game in France. "I put on my hunting clothes, put my gun over my shoulder and my game-bag on my back and set out for Clisson... A word of warning, in passing, for those Parisians who like to believe that the Vendée is a region where game is still abundant... I hunted there for a month and didn't even flush fifteen partridges." (*Mes Mémoires*, volume IV, 1830-1831).

Agreeing with an article which appeared in the *Vieux Chasseur*, Léon Bertrand feared that an additional cause of the disappearance of game was the spread of railways, which, bringing as they did an ever-increasing number of hunters to the countryside, "will soon complete the downfall of game in France". (*La chasse et les chasseurs*, 1862).

5. — WELL, WELL, WHAT ARE YOU DOING THERE, MR. CRUNICHON?... YOU DON'T EXPECT TO KILL ANYTHING SITTING DOWN ON THE GRASS, DO YOU?...
— WHY, YES INDEED... I AM IN THE PERFECT POSITION TO KILL TIME...

L. Delteil 2884, second state of three (in the third state the name is "Fumichon", instead of "Crunichon"). Plate No. 9 of the series *Emotions de chasse*. Published in *Le Charivari*, 18 September 1857.

The sketch of the two hunters is remarkable both for their attitudes and for the expressions Daumier has succeeded in putting on their faces. The rather fatuous air of superiority on the face of the one "who knows everything about hunting" contrasts amusingly with the tired bewilderment of his companion.

Characters such as these two are to be found described in contemporary texts. "The sluggish hunter is by no means the best, but he is the most agreeable; he is content with little, and with everything... The braggart hunts with his voice, and his voice does not ring true." *(Physiologie du chasseur)*. The braggart described in *Les Français peints par eux-mêmes*, is the double of Daumier's. "...This grotesque figure... the man who consents to encase his fat calves in leather gaiters and his "Lepeintre" stomach (Lepeintre was an actor renowned for his corpulence) in buckskin breeches, who has never bagged even the smallest of rabbits for as long as anyone can remember, and who when he gets home in the evening requires the assistance of his cook, his gardener and his eldest daughter to get out of the straitjacket of his hunting gear, while his wife directs operations, sponges his brow and calls him her great Nimrod." (Francis de Valrine, *Les Villas parisiennes*, 1841).

6. — I HAVE MADE MY MIND UP..., I SHALL NEVER HUNT WITH YOU AGAIN!...
— AND WHY NOT?
— MY FRIEND, YOU ARE SO UGLY YOU FRIGHTEN THE GAME AWAY!

L. Delteil 2606, second state of two. Plate No. 6 in the series *Emotions de chasse*. Published in *Le Charivari* at the end of 1854.

Overcome with heat and fatigue, angry at having bagged nothing, the hunters fall to insulting each other. Yet they seem to have done everything possible to turn the odds in their favour. Their hunting outfits are irreproachable and Daumier has taken a delight in showing us their every detail. Everything is there: the jacket, gaiters, hat, game-bag, powder-flask...

The hunting literature of the day was full of advice on hunting equipment.

René and Liersel (*New Treatise on hunting and fishing*, 1855) recommend "full garments, strong, waterproof foot-wear, gaiters... a cap, more convenient than a straw hat whose brim catches on branches. The pellet bag with a knee attachment is by far the most handy; the powder-flask should be equipped with a measure to ensure correct dosing of the charge... the satchel or game-bag should have dividing compartments in which each object should have its own place—a knife, a screwdriver, wadding paper, a spare box of primers, needle and thread, a small first aid kit, scissors, string, a cleaning-rag for the gun and, if desired, a small flask of liquor, not to mention the hunting licence which should always be readily available to show a game-keeper or policeman."

Joseph Vallée repeats the same advice concerning "the game-bag, that hunter's box of tricks", but adds a bottle of ammonia as a precaution against snake-bite. (*La chasse à tir en France*, 1854).

Le Journal des chasseurs (August 1837) doesn't "worry too much about hunting garb; dress yourself up as you see fit"; but it stresses "the host of accessories... percussion caps, wad extractors, priming needles... which are always essential in hunting."

Fashion engravings, published regularly in such magazines as *La Mode*, the *Petit courrier des dames*, and the *Journal des chasseurs* (clothes by Human, drawing by Gavarni, 1846), advised the fashionable hunter on his choice of outfit. "Twill jacket... with breast and hip pockets; trousers in dark check woollen twill; Spanish gaiters." More stylish were "the jacket in velvet, trousers in grey twill with diagonal stripes and close-fitting at the feet, a grey hat of smooth felt... a blue or black silk cravat knotted loosely around the neck..."

7. I SAW SOMETHING MOVE AT THE TOP OF THIS TREE... DO YOU THINK OUR RABBIT COULD HAVE CLIMBED UP THERE?

L. Delteil 2611, second state of two. Plate No. 11 of the series *Emotions de chasse*. Published in *Le Charivari* at the beginning of 1855.

Daumier has been particularly hard on these two wretched "weapon carriers" who imagine themselves to be hunters, and the expressions of stupidity and bewilderment he has put on their faces is quite remarkable.

But contemporary authors showed no greater tenderness for the so-called hunters "whose clumsiness is matched only by their ignorance". "Today, there are many who think they know everything merely because they have obtained a gun-licence from the prefecture... Hunting demands a whole host of anterior knowledge... The hunter who neglects these elementary notions will tire himself out unnecessarily and end up with nothing in his game-bag." (*Journal des chasseurs*, November 1841).

E. Blaze went even further. "Today landowners are renting out hunting rights to grocers. They are selling the right to kill hares and partridges to masons and tilers... to which can be added the baker, the tailor, the investor, the local merchant, and a whole new population which comes, on a regular day each week, to trample over the seigniorial lands..." (E. Blaze, *Le chasseur*, in *Les Français peints par eux-mêmes*, 1841).

8. — LISTEN... I SAW A HARE OVER THERE...
— WAS THAT A LONG TIME AGO?
— NOT AT ALL... LESS THAN THREE MONTHS AGO...

L. Delteil 2993, second state of two. Plate No. 2 of the series *Croquis de chasse* (a series of four drawings that appeared in *Le Charivari* between October 1857 and September 1858). Published on 2-3 November 1857.

The peasant's scorn for the townsman and his ignorance of the ways of the country was often a source of inspiration for Daumier's crayon (cf. also the two following plates). "A lot has been said of the foolishness of the provincial in Paris, but nothing has been written—and it is all wrong—about the crass ignorance displayed in the country by the Parisian who has never before emerged through the city gates... All he knows of animals and nature is what M. Buffon has condescended to tell him." (*Physiologie du Parisien en province*, 1841). "Generally speaking, the countryman cannot stand the city-dweller who comes out on Sunday and humiliates him by a display of the luxuriousness of his clothing; so, whenever they meet, he gladly seizes any opportunity to teach him a lesson." (*Physiologie du Bourgeois*, 1841). Recalling a shooting party, Alexandre Dumas notes in his *Mémoires* (1830): "We had all been obliged to pay the thousand and one little dues the peasants exact from the innocent hunter."

9. I SAW A HARE... (ASIDE) A WEEK AGO!

L. Delteil 1437, second state of two. Plate No. 50 of the

series *Pastorales* (a series of fifty plates that appeared in *Le Charivari* from May 1845 to May 1846). Published on 15 May 1846.

His wink and sly look confirm the peasant's satisfaction at playing a trick on this very naive novice hunter.

In looking at this plate it is interesting to note the care Daumier took, under the guise of apparent simplicity, to compose the elements of the countryside settings of his hunting and fishing scenes, although these are only the background to the main subject. According to Arsène Alexandre, "Daumier showed what an excellent landscape artist he was in his country and suburban scenes. How well he has understood and captured the spirit of the bare open countryside that surrounds Paris!... Those miserable clumps of trees, those contemptible little hills, those poplars that one comes across suddenly, standing isolated, for no particular reason, right in the middle of a field... all this is wonderfully portrayed in all its mediocrity; the artist has expressed in quite an extraordinary manner the character of this countryside, which is, precisely, to be quite character-less." (*Honoré Daumier,* 1888).

10. — LOOK MASTER, THAT LITTLE ONE HAS BEEN EATING UP ALL THE PRODUCE OF THE REGION. GIVE HIM A TASTE OF YOUR LEAD!
— I THINK IT'S A PHEASANT!

L. Delteil 2459, second state of two. Plate No. 11 of the series *Croquis de chasse*. (Series of twenty-one drawings, numbered haphazardly, that appeared in *Le Charivari* from October 1853 to February 1854). Published on 25 November 1853.

"This is the Parisian bourgeois who has declared war to the death on all the skylarks of the suburbs", says the *Journal Amusant* ironically in a column devoted to hunting.

This pinchbeck hunter advancing stealthily towards the "game-bird" pointed out to him by his tenant-farmer, is one of those Parisians who could never venture thirty miles from the capital, and contents himself with shooting at birds... one comes across those who take pleasure in shooting sitting birds in trees or on the ground." (*Physiologie du chasseur,* 1841).

The farmer, anxious for his crops, comes to ask the assistance of his master, because the shooting rights belong to the owner of the land and do not pass to the tenant-farmer.

But the farmers' protestations about the damage to crops caused by game drew upon them the anger of the author of the chapter on the *Country Policeman* in *Les Français peints par eux-mêmes* (1841): "The days have passed when game used to multiply and reduce the peasant to hunger... snares, traps, nets, the peasant uses any kind of weapon...

and he pursues every variety of game relentlessly; and each year the game becomes more rare."

This lithograph, and the ten following, are unusual in Daumier's work in that the characters are drawn with large heads, a style that was frequently used around 1853.

11. WHATEVER POSSESSED ME TO THINK OF COMING TO HUNT ON THESE DAMNED PLAINS OF SOLOGNE WHEN I DON'T KNOW THE REGION... I CAN'T FIND A FARM AND WILL HAVE TO SPEND THE NIGHT IN THE OPEN... WHAT A BORE! AT LEAST MY DOG CAN AMUSE HIMSELF BAYING AT THE MOON!

L. Delteil 2464, second state of three. Plate No. 7 of the series *Croquis de chasse*. Published in *Le Charivari* on 30 December 1853.

It seems clear from the starkness of the composition that Daumier had never set foot in Sologne. Or perhaps this just indicates the caption-writer's ignorance of the Sologne countryside, for it is known that Daumier very rarely wrote the captions for his drawings. If the artist or the caption-writer had read the chapter on the Sologne by Félix Pyat in *Les Français peints par eux-mêmes* (1841), there is some excuse for him. This is what he would have read: "There is a large area of France, consisting of about three Departments, which is called the Sologne. It is sandwiched, an oasis of sterility, between fertile provinces and the contrast is like that of evil beside good, poor beside rich. It is the French Siberia. A Parisian could be exiled to Sologne. The government, which seeks places of deportation beyond the seas to rid itself of its political prisoners, has only to send them to this desert, a bare thirty miles from Paris, where, as Charlet said of Egypt, the soil is sand, the air is a miasma, the water is a stagnant pond, and where it is impossible to live to a ripe old age..."

That great hunter Léon Bertrand's description is, luckily more accurate: "The soil is generally light and sandy and well suited to rabbits which, in spite of the enormous numbers that are slaughtered, are multiplying at an alarming rate. The arable land is sown with buckwheat, which is never harvested, and potatoes over which deer, stag and boar dispute... the meadows are swampy and the ponds are covered with reeds." (*La chasse et les chasseurs,* 1862).

12. NOCTURNAL FEARS.
WHAT A FOOL I WAS TO GO SO FAR CHASING RABBITS AND TO START BACK FOR HOME SO LATE... IS THAT A MAN... OR A TREE... I THINK IT IS TWO MEN.

L. Delteil 2451, second state of two. A plate from the series *Croquis de chasse*. Published in *Le Charivari* 20 October 1853.

The supposed dangers of hunting, the fears felt by the

bourgeois hunter, far away from his daily life and city background, and faced by an unknown and therefore hostile nature, inspired Daumier's artistry just as much as the themes of the hunter's ignorance and clumsiness (See also plates 29, 30, 31).

When Buffon wrote: "The warrior races, those who played an important role in world history, considered hunting as a pleasant schooling in the necessary art of war" *(Histoire Naturelle, Du Cerf)*, he ·certainly was not thinking of the type of hunter Daumier has depicted here.

13. A NOVICE HUNTER.
I THINK THAT IS A HARE... HOW THE DEVIL AM I SUPPOSED TO SHOOT IT?

L. Delteil 2455, second state of two. Plate No. 7 in the series *Croquis de chasse*. Published in *Le Charivari* on 10 November 1853.

"Today, now that there are no longer any great noblemen, everybody hunts. And to do this all that is necessary is to contribute the modest sum of 15 francs to the vast ocean of the budget." There is more than a little disdain in this remark made by E. Blaze (*Le Chasseur*, in *Les Français peints par eux-mêmes*, 1841), for he knew full well that there was more to it than this in knowing how to hunt.

If only this novice hunter had read the *Aphorismes de Saint Hubert* (all 111 of which appear at the end of the *Physiologie du chasseur*), before venturing out into the countryside, he would have been able to meditate on the truth of these lines:

"A hare runs to you, you must shoot at least
  A span in front, or you will miss the beast.
A hare runs from you, you must aim your shot
  Above his ears, he'll soon be in the pot."

Alexandre Dumas had no need of this advice when he found himself in a similar situation: "I had scarcely gone twenty paces across the clover field when a huge leveret started up under the dog's nose. Needless to say that leveret is dead." (*Mes Mémoires*, Volume IV, 1830).

14. THE DOG IS SAID TO BE MAN'S BEST FRIEND, BUT IS MAN ALWAYS REALLY THE DOG'S BEST FRIEND?...

L. Delteil 2615, second state of two. Plate No. 15 of the series *Emotions de chasse*. Published in *Le Charivari* 28 February 1855.

In this drawing Daumier takes up the classic story (he was to return to it many times) of the clumsy hunter who kills his own dog. This hunting classic has been handled by authors and artists of every period. Inevitably it was taken up in *La Physiologie du chasseur* (1841): "... the dog

rolled over in a pool of blood: a peasant of the region had fired at a jay in the undergrowth and had hit the dog".

The hunter's face is a picture of stupefaction mixed with consternation, as he stands in front of his dog to whom Daumier has given a skeleton-like quality, perhaps to heighten the contrast between the scene of death in the foreground and the flight of the hare, still very much alive, in the background.

15. AN UNLUCKY HUNTER AND A LUCKLESS DOG.

L. Delteil 2469, second state of two. Plate No. 22 of the series *Croquis de chasse*. Published in *Le Charivari*, 21 January 1854.

The clumsy hunter finds another way of killing his dog (cf. the previous drawing).

Where does the distinction lie between clumsiness and bad luck? Recording some of the comments made by some sportsmen among themselves during a shoot, *L'Hermite de la Chaussée d'Antin* (1841) notes this remark among others: "That fellow there can do nothing right; he is right out of luck (hunters, like gamblers, have their prejudices and superstitions)".

16. WHICH GOES TO SHOW THE ADVANTAGE OF HAVING A SPANIEL IF YOU ARE FOND OF HUNTING IN THE MARSHES.

L. Delteil 2456, second state of three. Plate No. 8 of the series *Croquis de chasse*. Published in *Le Charivari*, 17 November 1853.

The vicissitudes of hunting in the marshes are often noted in hunting literature contemporary with Daumier's drawings. René and Liersel commented on them in their *Nouveau Traité de la chasse et de la pêche* (1855): "... in this kind of hunting it is almost impossible to avoid suffering from the effects of rheumatism brought on by the humidity and from unexpected duckings which can, on occasions, result in a fortnight in bed". So too did Elzéar Blaze: "It is most agreeable when there are plenty of birds about... and altogether it would be most amusing if only one's hands and feet were not frozen". (*Les chasseurs au canard*, in *Le chasseur conteur ou les Chroniques de la chasse*, 1840). The charms of hunting over the marshes are even vaunted in one of the *Aphorismes de Saint-Hubert*, although its inconvenient aspects are not passed over in silence:

"Were it not for the pains, five years later so strong,
  The delights of marsh-hunting would be all my song."

The caption to this lithograph calls for one comment, there is nothing spaniel-like about the dog in it. Daumier, so careful over every other detail, can certainly never have seen a spaniel, nor indeed any other hunting dog. None of his dogs resembles any known type of hunting dog. Those he drew were all of indeterminate breed of the type he saw, no doubt, in the streets of Paris.

17. HOW TERRIBLE TO HAVE COME ACROSS THIS WILD BOAR... BUT FOR THIS TREE I WOULD BE IN TROUBLE... HE SEEMS TO BE THINKING THINGS OVER... I HOPE HE IS THINKING OF LEAVING.

L. Delteil 2457, second state of two. Plate No. 9 of the series *Croquis de chasse.* Published in *Le Charivari*, 21 November 1853.

Another Daumier lithograph depicts virtually the same scene (Delteil 2602): *My God... let's hope he doesn't uproot the tree,* cries the hunter perched in a tree as he sees a wild boar (a real one this time) come charging towards him.

It is, of course, ridiculous for our novice hunter to be so frightened of a pig that has wandered from a neighbouring farmyard, but the very erudite *Journal des chasseurs* could furnish him, perhaps, with an argument in extenuation. In it we read, under the signature of Léon Bertrand, that "the boar is very closely related to an unclean animal, in fact, it is clearly of the same species; and despite the opinion of certain authors who find some fairly significant differences in the external body structure of the boar and the pig... it must be admitted, to our great regret, that they are of the same lineage. Let us say rather that one is a wild animal and the other a domestic animal... Only a very experienced hunter could distinguish between the tracks of the two animals, and even the very best bloodhound handlers are sometimes deceived". (February 1837, *Le Sanglier*).

18. RUN TO EARTH.

L. Delteil 2453, second state of two. Plate from the series *Croquis de chasse.* Published in *Le Charivari*, 8 November 1853.

"You have met him walking along the hedgerows... in the middle of the fields; you have recognized him... by his half-military, half-civilian appearance, ... by his sabre, his badge, his three-cornered hat with its cockade... The country policeman roams unceasingly throughout the region entrusted to his care... Not only does he have to deal with poachers, those buccaneers of hunting, now he is involved with hunters." (*Le Garde Champêtre*, by François Coquille, in *Les Français peints par eux-mêmes*, 1841).

Round about 1860 the number of poachers was estimated at some 455,000, while the average number of hunting licences issued annually was 155,000 (*Journal de l'Aisne*, 13 September 1865). But the poacher was not the country

policeman's only worry; the hunter too caused him considerable trouble at times. "Among those who roam the plains with guns over their shoulders, there are perhaps as many who defy the gun-licensing laws as those who submit to them", declared E. Blaze (*Le Chasseur,* 1841). He also records these words of a friend of his: "If I were hunting on my own land, I would get only half as much pleasure as I do hunting on my neighbour's property. Fear of the gamekeeper kindles my blood, I get a kick out of it, and to add to this sensation, next year I shall probably not take out a gun licence... it would be so much more amusing". Much the same state of mind animates the "very distinguished hunter who does not like paying in his annual fifteen-franc fee at the prefecture..., he goes in fear of the gendarmes and the country policeman and he tries to avoid them, and to trick them when he does fall into their hands, and all this doubles his pleasure". *(Le chasseur conteur, ou les Chroniques de la chasse,* by E. Blaze, 1840).

Even Alexandre Dumas admits in his *Mémoires* (volume IV, 1830), with unconcealed satisfaction: "It was pointed out to me that the hunting season was not open; but my sole reply was that that was all the more reason to seek out the game... If any country policeman should appear... I should take care to outdistance him. Those who know how I can walk have no fears on that score".

What crime or crimes has our hunter committed? If he is a reader of the *Journal des chasseurs,* he probably knows that "The court of appeal recently ruled that only one fine may be imposed on anyone caught hunting on another man's property during the close season. Make the most of this". (In an article signed Nimrod).

Surveillance, however, because more and more strict and 20,778 persons were charged with game offences in 1865, as compared with 6,231 in 1836 and 8,093 in 1941 (E. Jullien, *La chasse, son histoire, sa législation,* 1868).

The law of 1844 which laid down a policy concerning hunting marked an important date in the history of the sport.

Intended mainly to suppress poaching and to ensure the conservation of game, the law of 1844 also clarified a number of other points and remained unchanged until 1874. It was widely commented on in magazines and books on hunting of the day, receiving, in general, a favourable reception among hunters. "May 3 marks the beginning of a new era in hunting, and the Minister of Justice deserves well of both the hunter and the game he pursues". (*Journal des chasseurs,* September 1844).

19. THE DIFFICULTY OF HUNTING IN A REGION WHERE THERE IS TOO MUCH GAME.

L. Delteil 2452, second state of two. A plate in the series

Croquis de chasse. Published in *Le Charivari*, 25 October 1853.

Pheasants? Partridges? Probably a covey of partridges, but we certainly cannot tell from Daumier's drawing and this is really rather surprising in him. This man, whose observation and whose crayon were normally so precise, was quite careless in his portrayal of game in all his hunting lithographs (cf. the hares in plates 24 and 30 and the game birds in plates 20, 22 and 34).

If any doubt about it remained, this lithograph would surely be the best proof that Daumier had never seen a covey of partridges take flight (otherwise his keen eye and infallible memory would have recorded it). He almost certainly had never gone hunting.

It is unusual to find among Daumier's caricatures on hunting, a drawing showing "too much game". The contrary is much more usual.

Perhaps he had heard people around him talking about, or had read an article praising, the benefits that would come from the famous law of 3 May 1844 (cf. the previous plate).

In the same year that the law was introduced, an article in the *Journal des chasseurs* (September 1844) announced enthusiastically that "the opening of the 1844 season signalled the wisdom and efficacy of the law of May 3. The future and the re-population of game in France was henceforth ensured. Coveys of as many as twenty-two partridges have been seen in the plain of Saint-Denis."

20. MR. PRUDHOMME GOES HUNTING.
— LOOK PAPA!... PARTRIDGE... SHOOT THEM!...
— NO, MY BOY... IF WE KILL THE PARTRIDGE THIS YEAR THERE WON'T BE ANY LEFT FOR NEXT SEASON.

L. Delteil 2879, second state of two. Plate No. 2 of the series *Emotions de chasse*. Published in *Le Charivari*, 24 November 1856.

The artist Cham, who also himself depicted Mr. Prudhomme hunting (*Les bons Parisiens*, 1855), credits him with similar sentiments: "I have been hunting now for twenty years, and I am proud to say that I have never fired a single shot and have not had a single drop of blood on my conscience throughout my whole sporting career".

The *Journal Amusant* (14 January 1860), shows *Mr. Prudhomme hunting* "... in the plain of Virtue... with a ferret and a formidable array of equipment... in six hours hunting all he hit was a few sparrows' feathers".

21. THE DISADVANTAGES OF SHOOTING PARTRIDGE WITH DEVISME'S NEW EXPLOSIVE BULLETS.

L. Delteil 2891, second state of two. Plate No. 17 of the

series *Emotions de chasse*. Published in *Le Charivari*, 14 September 1858.

Considerable progress was made in the manufacture of arms in the middle of the XIXth century. There were many discoveries and inventions relating both to weapons themselves and the ammunition for them.

In 1855, René and Liersel wrote: "So many more or less perfected hunting guns have been made, so many patents registered, that the variety of choice is almost too great... there remains the battle for supremacy between muzzle-loading percussion guns and breech-loading guns, and among the latter between those with a barrel-break and those in which only the breech-bolt moves". *(Nouveau Traité de la chasse et la pêche)*.

As early as 1841, the author of the *Physiologie du chasseur* noted that each gunsmith had his own invention and his own system... the gunsmiths of Paris deserve our praise... Perrin, Lepage, Patel senior, Delausse, Le Lion, Lefaure, André, Armand, Léon Pirmet, Prélat... the gunsmiths of Paris rank high in the industry".

Other names appear several times in books on hunting and articles of the time, and each writer explained his own preferences: "The Lefaucheux system (with breaking barrel, perfected in about 1850) has had the greatest success... but it entails carrying with one a large number of ready-made cartridges; at all events, with other weapons one has to carry power and pellets which weigh just as much."

Other names quoted included Béringer, Lefaucheux's successor, Robert (gold medal of 1834), and finally Devisme who, according to Léon Bertrand, is today "virtually the exclusive supplier of the real sportsmen of the provinces and of the capital". (*La chasse et les chasseurs*, 1862).

Exhibited among the weapons made by all the great names of contemporary arms manufacture, at the Museum of Hunting and of Nature, in Paris, is a carbine by Devisme that fires explosive bullets, for big-game hunting (about 1865).

Perhaps our hunter, on the target for once, had the unhappy notion of using one of these explosive projectiles, in no way intended for use against partridge.

At all events he succeeded in causing stupefaction (perhaps more disgust, for the woman) among these harmless people out for their Sunday walk. The man's posture and expression (he bears some resemblance to Mr. Prudhomme) are very similar to those of the hunter in the following drawing.

22. AH! I THINK THEY MUST BE BIRDS OF PREY... THEY WERE EATING GRAPES!

L. Delteil 1517, second state of two. Plate No. 41 of

the series *Les bons bourgeois*. Published in *Le Charivari*, 20 April 1847.

If he thinks that these are "birds of prey", this dumbfounded hunter must know that "One only hunts in the vineyards after the wine-harvest. The wine-grower doesn't want dogs eating his grapes, or the hunters, as they pass, plucking off the bunches, damaging the vines or breaking the vine-props." (Joseph La Vallée, *Chasse dans les vignes*, in *La chasse à tir en France*, 1854).

23. AND NOT A GRAIN OF POWDER LEFT!

L. Delteil 1730, second state of two. Plate No. 2 of the series *Quand on a du guignon*. (A series of 11 drawings, all but two of which appeared in *Le Charivari* from February 1848 to June 1850. Published on 22 February 1848.

The powder-flask was one of the essential items in the hunter's equipment. There was a great variety of models, not all of them safe. "Those in which the small measure that holds the charge remains in contact with the inside of the flask have one great disadvantage—if any powder remains alight in the barrel when you pour in the charge, your powder flask... will explode, presenting a grave threat to your hand. Other models offer greater security: when you pour the powder into the barrel, they are detached and isolated from the inside of the flask, so that there is less fear of an explosion". This, at any rate, was the opinion of Joseph La Vallée (*La chasse à tir en France*, 1854).

In their *Nouveau Traité de la chasse et de la pêche* (1855), René and Liersel give some practical advice on loading the gun and the making of cartridges. "Ammunition required for hunting is limited to a small stock of medium-grade powder—it is forbidden to obtain this from anyone except an authorized supplier—pellets of several calibres and some primers... With the gun in position, hammers down, the powder poured into the barrel, a first wad is inserted and tamped down hard; then the pellets are inserted which in turn are tamped down lightly with the aid of a second wad; only tamp a little to avoid mealing the power. The hammers are then raised and the primers inserted. The hammers are then carefully lowered as a safety measure...

As far as possible cartridges should be prepared in advance; this saves time and ensures that the charges are all the same".

The *Journal des Chasseurs* has some reservations on this point, because "the real difficulty with cartridges prepared in advance is that the amount of power placed in the barrel cannot be varied according to circumstances (dryness or humidity of the air, etc.). (*Des armes de jet employées à la chasse*, September 1837).

Concerning the amount of powder to be used, Joseph La Vallée gives a precise indication: "The biggest charge that can usefully be used should, before it is tamped down, fill the barrel to a height one and a half times its diameter. Any additional power will give no increase in range".

"A gun over-charged spits out fire and flame,
But a charge that's too weak won't kill any game."
(*Aphorismes de Saint-Hubert*)

24. A MISPLACED SHOT.
HOW ONE CAN EXPERIENCE THE MOST LIVELY EMOTIONS EVEN IN THE CALM OF THE COUNTRYSIDE.

L. Delteil 1398, second state of three. Plate No. 11 of the series *Pastorales*. Published in *Le Charivari*, 1 July 1845 (3rd state).

"Don't fire your gun towards human faces
Though they be far from you, even three hundrer paces",
(*Aphorismes de Saint-Hubert*).

Alphonse Herr (*Dictionnaire du pêcheur*, 1855) states, with a touch of irony, that as a pastime hunting is "rather expensive; furthermore it is dangerous. Each year, a month after the season opens, one notes with sadness that more hunters than partridges have been killed".

It will be noted that the hare in the drawing bears very little resemblance to the animal as it really is (cf. plate 19).

25. GOOD HEAVENS!... AND I THOUGHT I'D BAGGED A RABBIT...

L. Delteil 2883, second state of two. Plate No. 8 of the series *Emotions de chasse*. Published in *Le Charivari*, 19 September, 1857.

The blunder committed by this character, who must surely be one of those "grocer-hunters who kill anything" (*Le chasseur*, 1841), provides Daumier with the opportunity to give us a fine composition. The hunter's posture, his astonishment vying with curiosity and incredulity, the dog's pride at finding and bringing back the quarry, the countryside with the house half hidden in a clump of trees, the gesticulations of the woman running towards the hunter and the promise of a lively confrontation to come, all this could not be better summed up than by those so appropriate words of Claude Roger-Marx: "Daumier is at his best depicting the trivial. With him an anecdote becomes a drama". (*L'Univers de Daumier*, 1972). Note also the quality of the light which Daumier expresses here in an exceptionally beautiful way. Claude Roger-Marx points out that "Daumier's use of black has been rightly praised. But what are we to say of his transparent greys and, above all, of his rich, brilliant, almost miraculous whites, so varied that he seems to have at his disposal a whole palette of colours".

26. — LOOK, I HAVE JUST BAGGED THIS MAGNIFICENT GROUSE!...
— STUPID!... THAT IS THE COCK FROM THE FARMYARD OVER THERE... THAT COCK IS GOING TO COST YOU AT LEAST THIRTY FRANCS... NOT TO MENTION A FEW BLOWS WITH A PITCHFORK!...

L. Delteil 3216, second state of three. Plate No. 6 of the series *Croquis de chasse.* (Series of seven drawings that appeared in *Le Charivari* from September to November 1859). Published on 31 October 1859.

Note the pride of the hunter as he awaits the congratulations of his companion. The latter, however, shows only his consternation. (See plate No. 36 concerning the fine imposed for this type of offence).

How far we have come, with this ironical caricature, from "what is properly called hunting..., that pastime of the civilized nations which consists of pursuing wild animals, deliberately maintained in that state." (*Chasses et amusements nationaux de la Grande-Bretagne,* by H. Alken, 1821).

The house to be seen behind the big white wall is perhaps the same one that appears in the following drawing, in which the wall assumes a greater importance. Perhaps it was a friend's house where Daumier and his wife went to take their Sunday rest.

27. JUST LOOK AT THAT!... WHEN I DO KILL A PARTRIDGE... IT FALLS IN MY NEIGHBOUR'S GARDEN!

L. Delteil 3214, second state of two. Plate No. 4 of the series *Croquis de chasse. Published in Le Charivari,* 10 October 1859.

Although the partridge seen falling is not particularly realistic, Daumier has given us here a magnificent drawing; what a wonderful sense of composition he demonstrates as he makes play with the vertical lines of the hunter and his dog against the big wall.

Had he known the law, the hunter would not have been so downcast. He would have been aware that game belongs to the man who kills it and that he has the right to enter his neighbour's property to collect it provided he takes certain precautions, such as unloading his gun or, better still, leaving it at the entrance, so as not to commit the offence of entering armed into another person's territory.

28. SO I HAVE BAGGED A PARTRIDGE!... OH, NO, ITS A SPARROW!

L. Delteil 3468, second state of two. Plate No. 2 of the

series *Croquis de chasse.* (Series of six drawings that appeared in *Le Charivari* in October' and November 1864). Published on 19 October.

The peasant makes no attempt to conceal his contemptuous glee at the discomfiture of the hunter from the city, the spiritual brother of the one who aroused the mockery of *L'Hermite de la Chaussée d'Antin,* (1814). "The love of the hunt is parodied in Paris in the most amusing way by some members of the middle-classes. Can you imagine anything more grotesque than the worthy grocer of the Rue de la Verrerie, whose house is guarded by a gun-dog, and who, raising himself above the level of his family's vulgar pleasures, looks forward to Sundays when he goes out into the fields, where he may succeed in killing a lark or a wagtail?"

29. A CREATURE MUST BE STUPID TO MAKE YOU SO AFRAID!...

L. Delteil 2609, second state of two. Plate No. 9 of the series *Emotions de la chasse.* Published in *Le Charivari,* 9 December 1854.

On several occasions Daumier showed us timid hunters frightened by imaginary dangers (cf. plates 12, 30 and 31). The fear of animals, in particular of the hare and the rabbit, itself a timid animal if ever there was one, inspired him to a number of delightful drawings. "Theodore, be careful!" (Delteil 2468) says a wife to her husband on spotting a rabbit, "wild animals are nearly always ferocious beasts!" "What the devil can that be there in that thicket?" the puzzled hunters ask. "Perhaps it is a tiger" (Delteil 2610). "Be careful, my friend, that animal could be very dangerous" (Delteil 2892): a man and a woman, out for their Sunday walk, are bending over a rabbit. Transformed by Daumier's imaginative genius, this is a version of the classic story of "the hunter hunted".

R. Escholier has given an excellent description of that "worthy, mediocre person, the lower middle-class Parisian. A tradesman from the city in the heart of the suburban wastes... his instinctive horror of the countryside and nature frightens the animals that inhabit it..." (*Daumier et son monde,* 1965).

30. IN WHICH WE SEE THAT IT IS NOT ALWAYS VERY PLEASANT WHEN A HARE STARTS UP UNDER YOUR FEET.

L. Delteil 2614, second state of two. Plate No. 14 of the series *Emotions de chasse.* Published in *Le Charivari,* 15 January 1855.

The instinctive movement of recoil of the hunter in the previous drawing is here taken to the extreme, that is to say, to the point that the hunter falls. What strength and movement there is in this caricature!

The *Journal des Chasseurs* had not, of course, foreseen a situation such as this when it gave advice on shooting hare. However, it advises the hunter to be very alert: "In the open plain one should never miss a hare that makes a bolt for it within easy range. Yet they often are missed, and this is because the hunter was not on his guard... It is at the moment when one least expects it that the hare breaks cover." (September 1837).

To the discomfiture of the fall is added for this hunter the chagrin of missing a fine animal, for "though the grocer-hunter hunts in part for the pleasure of the sport, he hopes that his bag will compensate somewhat for the time he has spent, the powder he has used and the shoes he has worn. A hare running through the woods for him is nothing more that a franc piece on four legs." (E. Blaze, *Le Chasseur*, in *Les Français peints par eux-mêmes*, 1841).

31. WHY DOES THAT BEAST KEEP FOLLOWING ME... I'D GLADLY PAY SIX SOUS TO BE ABLE TO GET ON A BUS!...

L. Delteil 2601, second state of two. Plate No. 1 of the series *Emotions de chasse*. (A series of fifteen drawings that appeared in *Le Charivari* from October 1854 to February 1855). Published on 10 November 1854.

Fear is once again the subject of this strange composition. This time it really is a question of "the hunter hunted". The hunter's fear is compounded by that of the dog who slinks along, ears back, his tail between his legs. These two make up an exceptionally well drawn group that, with a few clumps of comforting vegetation, occupies only the left hand side of the drawing, in sharp contrast with the right hand side in which the starkness of the countryside increases the terror engendered by the presence of "that beast" which is, perhaps, a wolf; unless, that is, it is no more than a stray dog.

But perhaps on this occasion the hunter's fear was justified and did not deserve this ironical treatment. Wolves were in fact, still common in France in the middle of the xixth century. Many articles, especially in the *Journal des Chasseurs*, make reference to them. "Woman fights off a she-wolf" (according to *La feuille de Saumur*, January 1837). In the Aveyron, "on the second day of the Easter holiday, there was a mass wolf-hunt..."; "on the 22nd of March, at Amoustie, in the Meuse, two wolves and three she-wolves were taken. Mr. Guiot succeeded in killing two with one shot from his gun and a third with his second shot." (*Journal des Chasseurs*, April 1837). *Le Vosgien*, the newspaper of Neufchâteau, reported that a shepherd had captured and killed a wolf that had stolen several sheep.

And even quite near Paris, "the people who live on the outskirts of the forests of Saint-Germain and Villefermoy have been complaining of the ravages caused by wolves and wild boar." (*Journal des Chasseurs*, August 1837).

It was not unusual for boar and wolf shoots to be organized after the close of the hunting season.

The *Journal des Chasseurs* (which appeared until 1870) each year gave "An account of the number of dangerous or harmful animals destroyed by vermin extermination officers in the course of their duties during the season". An impressive number of wolves figure on these lists.

32. A HUNTER MUST KEEP HIS SELF-RESPECT.
HERE'S WHAT YOU WANT... HOW ABOUT A FINE GOOSE TO GO WITH IT?... I COULD LET YOU HAVE A SUPERB LOBSTER!...

L. Delteil 2465, second state of two. Plate No. 18 of the series *Croquis de chasse*. Published in *Le Charivari*, 5 January 1854.

One must at all costs avoid the shame of returning emptyhanded. "This is the moment when the unsuccessful hunter decides to go to the Palais-Royal and to hunt there, purse in hand, among the food shops. There he purchases a brace of partridge which he places in his game-bag. When he brings the birds out later he takes care to ensure that their claws are entangled in the meshes of his net." (*L'Hermite de la Chaussée d'Antin*, 1814).

In his preface to A. Rossel's book, *Daumier : Emotions de chasse* (1973), Mr. de Linarès quite rightly points out that whereas Daumier's representations of weapons, dogs and live game are "flagrantly inaccurate"—clear proof that he never hunted himself—"his dead game hanging in the shop is sketched to perfection; he had seen it for himself in the local grocery."

The style of this drawing shows certain links with those showing characters with large heads (cf. plates 10 to 19).

33. — HEY THERE, MY GOOD MAN! HOW MUCH DO YOU WANT FOR YOUR HARE?
— FOUR FRANCS.
— I'LL GIVE YOU FIVE IF YOU WILL HOLD IT UP LIKE THAT AND LET ME SHOOT AT IT!...

L. Delteil 3306, second state of two. Plate No. 3 of the series *Croquis de chasse*. Published in *Le Charivari*, 20 October 1864.

The scene portrayed here by Daumier is very similar to the one described by E. Blaze (*Le Chasseur*, in *Les Français peints par eux-mêmes*, 1841). "A man who has left his house in the morning before dawn and who returns in the evening tired out and ravenous, cannot with decency come back emptyhanded... So, on an occasion like that, any hunter with five francs in his pocket will rejoin his household with at least a brace of partridge."

Once again the talent with which Daumier handles the effects of light is to be noted here. We sense the intense luminosity of this sunny day, not only because of the heavily emphasized shadow of the hunter, but also because of the deliberately hazy outline of the peasant, whose silhouette is blurred by the light.

34. OVER-COURTEOUS HUNTERS.
— IS MADAME COQUELET WELL?...
— YOU ARE VERY KIND... HAS YOUR AUNT RECOVERED FROM HER COLD?
— COMPLETELY RECOVERED... AND HOW ARE YOU THESE DAYS?... ETC... (IN THE MEANTIME THE PARTRIDGE TOO ARE ENJOYING THE BEST OF HEALTH).

L. Delteil 2605, second state of two. Plate No. 5 of the series *Emotions de chasse*. Published at the end of 1854.

Deyeux, the author of the *Physiologie du chasseur* (1841) was himself a great hunter and, indeed, had lost a hand in a hunting accident. He could not fail, therefore, to be incensed by the lack of passion and interest in the sport exhibited by certain hunters. He poked fun at them in a spirit very similar to that of Daumier. "... everyone discusses the results achieved. A thousand comments, a thousand lies, a thousand stories are exchanged. And while all this talking is going on, the partridge fly away and not a shot is fired, so busy are they all with what they have done instead of with what remains to be done."

And "look at those two hunters walking along by this wood and talking about the pretty women of Paris, dawdling along with their guns reversed on their shoulders, while a hare starts up under their feet."

35. POLITENESS TAKEN TO THE EXTREME.
WHEN HUNTERS ASK ABOUT EACH OTHERS HEALTH THE HARES FLOURISH (APHORISM, SAINT-HUBERT).

L. Delteil 2992, second state of three. Plate No. 1 of the series *Croquis de chasse*. Published in *Le Charivari*, 30 October 1857.

Another scene of exaggerated politeness, of social gossip, very similar to the preceding drawing, although Daumier has taken the subject up again several years later.

Once again one is tempted to ask why these two men who seems so uninterested in the game so near at hand bother to go hunting. The answer is to be found perhaps in *La Physiologie du Chasseur*: "*A gentleman who goes hunting for the sake of his health...* in fact, he rarely goes hunting, but often goes for a walk with his gun, bringing back some English pears or a wounded partridge."

The craze for hunting inspired Deyeux to write a poem entitled *La Chassomanie*.

36. — SIR, IN VIEW OF THE COMPLETE ABSENCE OF GAME WOULD YOU ALLOW ME TO SHOOT AT YOUR DOG?
— SIR, I WAS ABOUT TO MAKE YOU THE SAME PROPOSITION!...

L. Delteil 3460, second state of two. Plate No. 4 of the series *Croquis d'automne*. (A series of six drawings that appeared in *Le Charivari* in September and October 1865). Published on 26 September.

The caption-writer—it will be recalled that the captions were very rarely written by Daumier—wanted to give a somewhat different sense to this scene which, like the two preceding ones, represents an exchange of courtesies between two hunters who meet. The features of the character on the left are surprisingly like those of Daumier himself. Could it be that he wanted to portray himself, just for once in the costume of one of these hunters, one of whose number he never was, but whom he had so often drawn? In that case the caption could well have read simply: "Good morning, Mr. Daumier". Perhaps all that lies behind this innocent mystification is that he wanted to pay a small tribute to himself, to his own talent and to his hunters.

To return to the caption, of course, neither of these two hunters has the slightest intention of carrying through with the proposal put to the other. But *Journal des Chasseurs* informs us that "many people seem to think they have the right to shoot at a dog they discover hunting their land; hounds are often victims of this popular error. Article 479 of the penal code inflicts a fine of 11 to 15 francs on anyone who, by use of arms or the throwing of stones occasions the death or wounding of animals or beasts belonging to another." (September 1937, *Legal cases*).

Another article gives an account of a judgement made by the municipal tribunal of Creil-sur-Oise: "... it is permissible to kill rabbits, but to kill a neighbour's dog on the grounds that he has trespassed on private land is against the law."

37. ONCE I SPOT A HARE IT IS AS GOOD AS DEAD... AND MY DOG... WHAT A WONDERFUL NOSE!...

L. Delteil 3304, second state of two. Plate No. 1 of the series *Croquis de chasse*. Published in *Le Charivari*, 13 October 1864.

Just a braggart, like Tartarin? (*Tartarin de Tarascon* was to be published in 1872). Or a "theoretical hunter", like the one described by E. Blaze? "He was a type apart; he never did any harm to the game because he never did any hunting... all he did was to talk hunting all day." (*Le Chasseur*, in *Les Français peints par eux-mêmes*, 1841).

There is an altogether admirable realism about even the minutest details of this conversation: the postures of the characters, the sly self-satisfied air of the man on the left, the gestures of his hands, the admiring, somewhat envious interest of the man on the right, their hunting outfits complete with game-bags and powder-flasks which seem to underline their lack of interest in what is going on around them, the placidity of the dog whose wonderful sense of smell is apparently unaffected by the close proximity of the hare.

38. A HUNTING YARN.
THE HUNTER: JUST THEN A HARE STARTED UP TO MY RIGHT... BANG! I KILLED HIM... THE SHOT DISTURBED A COVEY OF PARTRIDGES TO MY LEFT... BANG! I BAGGED THREE OF THEM!... A WILD DUCK FLEW OVER MY HEAD... BANG! AND DOWN IT CAME.
THE LISTENER: (ASIDE) WELL, WELL... HE MUST HAVE A TRIPLE-BARRELLED GUN!

L. Delteil 3307, second state of three. Plate No. 4 of the series *Croquis de chasse*. Published in *Le Charivari*, 29 October 1864.

"The hunter is a liar!" the *Physiologie du chasseur* affirms categorically; "this is the view generally and proverbially accepted." It is true that "hunting yarns", like "fishing yarns" (cf. plate 46), are classic subjects for jokes. Daumier, of course, could not neglect this topic, and with what zest he attacks it! The exaltation of the storyteller, who combines word and gesture, is accentuated by the extraordinary lighting effect which cuts the composition diagonally in two. His corpulent figure and his animated face contrast with the expressions of astonishment and incredulity on the faces of his companions.

In the same spirit E. Blaze remarked ironically: "Look at all these gentlemen; they sometimes lie when recounting their hunting adventures, but they do it in such a way that people believe them, or at least, pretend to believe them." (*Le Chasseur conteur*, 1840).

B. H. Revoil was not taken in by them either. "I have often heard hunters explaining how skilled they were and recounting their feats, but as I listened to their boastings I was laughing up my sleeve." (*Bourres de fusil*, 1865).

The *Journal des Chasseurs* concludes: "In no country in the world is as much game killed as at Tortoni's, at the Café Anglais, at the Opera or at the Italiens." (September 1837, *Habillement du Chasseur*).

39. IT'S VERY OLD, THE FISH HAVE STOPPED BITING FOR THE LAST TWO HOURS!

L. Delteil 312, second state of four, 1840, with the title: *Chasse et pêche No. 11*, replacing the title of the series: *La Chasse No. 11* (First state, published in *Le Charivari* on 18 January 1837). Published again in *Le Chaos...*, plate No. 4, 1840, with the caption: *One way of cooling the*

ardour of his passions; and in the *Nouvelle lanterne magique*, 24, 1845.

What was the general opinion about fishing, in France, in the middle of the XIXth century? As for hunting, Daumier's drawings, with all their jibes and mockeries, are a precious source of information which finds confirmation in contemporary texts and commentaries.

"It is clear that a man is born a hunter or an angler... Fishing was the first of man's skills; except in the case of a few big landowners, hunting today offers little pleasure, at least in France." This, at any rate, was the opinion of Alphonse Karr (*Dictionnaire du pêcheur*, 1855), and he added that after being a fisherman and then a hunter, "man was obliged to become a farmer; and these are the only three occupations worthy of a lofty soul."

Alexandre Dumas felt a kinship with all his "hunting and even his fishing colleagues". He praised the merits of "these two great arts which have the advantage over all the others of being also amusements." (Preface to *Vive la chasse*, by B.H. Revoil, 1867).

"Although I am a hunter, I like fishing very much", admitted Revoil. "Isn't fishing a form of hunting?" (*Bourres de fusil*, 1865).

This was also the opinion of the author of the *Physiologie du chasseur* (1841) for whom, "Fishing is hunting in water."

In the advance notice for their *Nouveau Traité de la chasse et de la pêche* (1855), René and Liersel explain to their readers the advantages of both these sports. "Whereas hunting, which is preferred by younger people, develops one's physical strength, inures the body to fatigue and is more apt than any other sport to produce healthy generations, fishing is more suitable for those who have retired from business and are fatigued by the noise of the city. It demands patience and sharpens the mind since it calls for a study of the habits and customs of the many forms of water life; just as much as hunting, fishing demands a precision and skill undreamt of by those who are pleased to ridicule a pastime with many attractions for those who address themselves to it with taste and perseverance."

We learn also of a much older testimony to the merits of fishing: "Suetonius tells us that to chase away the cares and boredom of the throne, Augustus used to go fishing with a rod and line." (Ameilhon, after Littré).

This first plate on fishing, like that on hunting, is a copy of a caricature by Seymour (cf. plate 1). The composition is exactly the same, the only changes being in the details of the dress of the man and the boy. In Seymour's original drawing the English angler is wearing a riding jacket and a hat and the child is wearing an English school hat, details which would have come as something of a surprise to the French public.

40. HAVE PITY ON A POOR FISHERMAN (Translator's note: In French there is a play on words and the caption could equally read "Have pity on a poor sinner").

L. Delteil 524, second state of two. Plate No. 2 of the series *Cours d'histoire naturelle* (a series of twelve numbered drawings that appeared in *Le Charivari* from December 1837 to October 1838). Published on 15 March 1838.

More even than in his hunting caricatures, Daumier stressed the *boredom* of rod and line fishing, to which was often added the unpleasantness of bad weather.

Daumier's anglers are the blood-brothers of his hunters. Lower middle-class Parisians, they come regularly to bore themselves along the banks of the Seine or, on Sundays, beside the rivers of the suburbs.

But yet how different they are! Daumier's anglers are much more humble than his hunters. Perhaps it is merely due to the difference in dress—there is a "hunting outfit" which enables the hunter to take himself more seriously perhaps, but there is no equivalent "fishing outfit". This poor fisherman, standing motionless under the driving rain, is, it is true, in a particularly wretched state. But thanks to him Daumier has given us a fine view of the quays of Paris with its old houses all of different sizes, which in itself is a valuable record.

If we are to believe M. J. Brisset, *The fisherman on the banks of the Seine* is the happiest of mortals: "Like the poet, he forgets worldly things. Lost in the shadow of the arches of these magnificent bridges and sheltered by the stone of the quays... the angler on the banks of the Seine cares little for the hubbub of the revolutions taking place above his head." (In *Les Français peints par eux-mêmes*, 1841).

41. THE OLD FISHERMAN.
THE ANGLER IS AN INDEPENDENT-MINDED, PERSEVERING, UN-COMPLAINING MAN WHO IS NOT DISCOURAGED BY ADVERSITY AND BATTLES AGAINST ALL THE DIFFICULTIES THAT ENCOMPASS HIM, SUFFERING STORM AND TEMPEST IN PHILOSOPHICAL SILENCE.

L. Delteil 571, second state of two. Plate 13 of the series *Types Parisiens*. Published in *Le Figaro*, 15 September 1839, and then in *Le Charivari*, 10 July 1841.

Types Parisiens is a series of fifty numbered plates published in *Le Charivari*. Plates Nos. 1 to 41 had appeared earlier (in *La Caricature provisoire* or *Le Figaro*), sometimes under different titles. A wide variety of subjects were dealt with under the general title of *Types Parisiens*.

To the question: why do people go fishing? (a question one is reasonably entitled to ask), the texts provide a variety of answers. "The man who fishes because he has nothing better to do is just another type of idle saunterer. The idler, tired of idling, goes fishing; for him fishing is a kind of rest, or, if you prefer, a kind of idler's retreat." (*Le pêcheur des bords de Seine,* by Brisset).

"For this kind of man, fishing is the absence of anything bad rather than the presence of a particular pleasure; he scarcely gives a thought to the fish to be caught, he thinks instead that his wife is not there. He savours this moment of repose and breathes in tranquillity through every pore." (Id.).

42. — DON'T YOU THINK WE OUGHT TO BE GOING?...
— HORTENSE, I THINK THEY ARE GOING TO START BITING... JUST HALF AN HOUR MORE.

L. Delteil 1549, second state of three. Plate 73 of the series *Le Bons Bourgeois* (a series of eighty-two drawings most of which appeared in *Le Charivari* between May 1846 and June 1849). Published in *Le Charivari*, 28 October 1847.

"Aphorism: fishing is a pleasure, even when you don't catch any fish." (Alphonse Karr, *Dictionnaire du pêcheur...,* 1855).

This is certainly not the view of this unfortunate woman as she stands soaked to the skin and paralysed with the cold (as for the man, he is almost smiling). But, like her comrade in misfortune of the following caricature, she "must follow her husband wherever he goes...".

And therein lies an important difference as compared with the hunting scenes in which no women figure. Hunting is the preserve of men. "In France, women have a very strong aversion to this form of amusement which they consider to be destructive of all social activity, all conversation and all sentiment. Furthermore, it accustoms men to seek, far from their sides, those pleasures in which they are unable to share." Perhaps the women of France would also have preferred not to be invited to share in the tediousness of rod and line fishing.

43. A WOMAN MUST FOLLOW HER HUSBAND WHEREVER HE ELECTS TO ESTABLISH HIS DOMICILE (CIVIL MARRIAGE CODE).

L. Delteil 1692, second state of two. Plate No. 46 of the series *Tout ce qu'on voudra.* (A series of seventy drawings most of which appeared in *Le Charivari* from March 1847 to July 1851). Published in *Le Charivari*, 31 May 1848.

Daumier's contemporaries agreed with him about the activities of the Parisian lower middle-classes: "... on Sundays they devote themselves to the pleasures of fishing." (*Physiologie du Bourgeois*, 1841).

The small investor, who figured in drawings by Chagot

and Beguin in the *Journal pour rire* (11 September 1852)..., *devoted himself on Sundays to the sweet delights of fishing.*

The hero of Daumier's caricature bears some resemblance to a man described by Maupassant in one of his short stories. "The day before he was due, for the first time in his life, to cast a hook in a river, Mr. Patissot bought himself, for the sum of 80 centimes, a copy of the *Perfect rod and line fisherman*. Then he went to join the other anglers each with his long, tapering rod, like pilgrims of old returning from Palestine." (*Les Dimanches d'un bourgeois de Paris* — pêche à la ligne).

44. MY DEAR, I'VE GOT A BITE... I'VE GOT A BITE!

L. Delteil 1501, second state of two. Plate No. 25 of the series *Les Bons Bourgeois*. Published in *Le Charivari*, 24 November 1846.

For Alphonse Karr, fishing had greater attractions to offer than hunting, for "when one does not make a kill, hunting means fatigue without pleasure;... fishing, however, would be a wonderful pleasure even if there were no fish in the world." (*Dictionnaire du pêcheur*, 1855). But when they are biting, it is "then that the anguish, the quickened heartbeats, the emotions arising from the most gripping drama of all, begin, to take possession of us. Do you know what I mean? "A bite'! the whole nature of the pleasure of fishing is summed up in those two words... for fishing is a pleasure in which the imagination plays the major role, a pleasure which, as a consequence, is closed to the cold practical mind." (*Le pêcheur des bords de Seine*, 1841).

Unlike the previous drawings, this scene evokes no feeling of tedium, on the contrary, it exudes a lot of charm. The fisherman's wife is with a friend with whom she has all the time in the world to gossip, the weather is fine, the countryside is agreeable, and what is more "they are biting". Once again Daumier shows his mastery of light and the delicate interplay of light and shadow.

Where is this scene located? No doubt somewhere in the suburbs of Paris. In his *Dictionnaire de la pêche* (1855), Alphonse Karr describes one such suburb. "Saint-Ouen, with its islands, its narrow little rivers from whose banks the willows trail their branches..." He also recalls having caught "some fine gudgeon off the tip of the Ile de Clichy... and heaven only knows how many crayfish I have had at Palaiseau in the Yvette."

45. WHAT PLEASURE CAN THEY GET OUT OF STANDING THERE LIKE THAT BY THE RIVER FOR FOUR HOURS AT A TIME?... AT LEAST I PLAY DOMINOES TO PASS THE TIME!...

L. Delteil 1704, second state of two. Plate No. 58 in the series *Tout ce qu'on voudra*. 1850. *Not published in Le Charivari.*

This is the answer to this "dominoes player's" question. "Vilify fishing who cares to, call a rod a pole with a creature on one end and an imbecile on the other, if you like, I take my stand against these detractors of this innocent pleasure... I admit that I have at times been one of those imbeciles, but a thousand wonderful memories remain with me of those hours spent with arms outstretched, my eye fixed on the float." (Brisset, *Le pêcheur des bords de Seine*, 1841).

Gide relates that his "principal occupation at la Roque... was fishing... My mother was very sad to see that I had such a taste for an amusement which, in her opinion, gave me too little exercise and wasted too much of my time. And I used to protest against the reputation fishing had acquired of being a dullard's sport." (*Si le Grain...*).

As for Whistler, he hated the countryside, but bowed to custom. "Like any self-respecting Englishman, I must do something; we shall go fishing for gudgeon, sitting in deck-clairs at the water's edge, and we shall watch the little red floats bobbing on the water." (*Whistler,* by Pennel, 1913).

46. A DIFFICULT SITUATION IN THE ANGLING CLUB.
— A BITE, WHAT LUCK!...
— I FORBID YOU TO CATCH A FISH BEFORE I DO, DON'T FORGET I AM YOUR VICE-PRESIDENT.

L. Delteil 3472, second state of two. Published in *Le Charivari*, 31 January 1866.

A minor drama is being played out between the two anglers in the foreground. The first angler is torn between the emotions of joy at getting a "bite"—in his excitement he half rises from his folding stool—and apprehension at the thought of upsetting his club vice-president. The latter, a wonderfully successful caricature, has something of the air, adopted perhaps as appropriate for a man with such important functions, of a typical English gentleman.

He is certainly in no doubt as to the importance of his role as vice-president, which consists primarily in ensuring that the laws of fishing are respected. Up to the Revolution, fishing, like hunting, was considered to be the prerogative of the land-owning nobility. However, the *Laws and Ordinances concerning Fishing* state that "formerly, the clergy were granted the right to fish, since there was something more humble about fishing than hunting, which they had always been forbidden to practice."

Should the angler with the stool lose his fish, he would still be able to tell a good tale about it. "The fish that gets away never weighs less than half a pound. It is a curious species that is noted for its very rapid growth. By evening it weighs a pound and in a week's time it will have become a monster-fish." (Alphonse Karr, *Dictionnaire du pêcheur,* 1855).

47. VIEW OF THE SEINE AT CHATOU...

L. Delteil 1716, second state of two. Last plate of the series *Tout ce qu'on voudra.* Published in *Le Charivari,* 19 July, 1851.

The accuracy of the scene depicted by Daumier is confirmed by Brisset. "During the fine season, the banks of the Seine are black, from morning till night, with anglers of all ages, shapes and sizes and dressed in every conceivable garb." (*Le pêcheur des bords de Seine,* 1841).

A little later Maupassant also added his testimony. "At Bezons, the river came into sight. On either bank a line of people, men in frock coats, twill jackets or blouses, women and children... were fishing." *(Contes : Les Dimanches d'un bourgeois de Paris. Pêche à la ligne).*

Daumier has given us here a wonderful composition, remarkable for the skill of the drawing and the use he has made of light. The angler in the foreground, shown sitting and seen from behind, reminds one of a sketch by Monet.

48. HERE'S A MAN WHO COMES FISHING AT THIS SPOT EVERY DAY FROM MORNING TILL NIGHT. I MUST FIND OUT HIS ADDRESS AND SEE IF HE HAS A PRETTY WIFE.

L. Delteil 3532, second state of two. Published in *Le Charivari,* 30 October, 1866.

From 1846 to 1863, Daumier lived at number 6 Quai d'Anjou. He was therefore very familiar with the life of the quays of Paris, and from his window he had a view "under his eyes of the bend in the little branch of the Seine... Anglers standing motionless with their rods and lines... All this against a background of the white, red and grey houses of the Quai des Célestins with their uneven roofs and irregularly placed windows." (Gustave Geoffroy, in R. Escholier, *Daumier et son monde,* 1965).

Alphonse Karr recalls with a certain nostalgia the expeditions he used to make when "escaping in the evening from the *pension* in the Rue Saint Anne, in Paris," he used to go fishing "on the banks of the Seine near the Vigier baths, after passing by the Carrousel."